T0163429

PRACTICALLY PAGAN

AN ALTERNATIVE
GUIDE TO COOKING

PRACTICALLY PAGAN

An Alternative
Guide to Cooking

Rachel Patterson

MOON
BOOKS

Winchester, UK
Washington, USA

JOHN HUNT PUBLISHING

First published by Moon Books, 2020
Moon Books is an imprint of John Hunt Publishing Ltd., No. 3 East Street, Alresford
Hampshire SO24 9EE, UK
office@jhpbooks.net
www.johnhuntpublishing.com
www.moon-books.net

For distributor details and how to order please visit the 'Ordering' section on our website.

ISBN: 978 1 78904 379 2
978 1 78904 380 8 (ebook)
Library of Congress Control Number: 2019945282

A CIP catalogue record for this book is available from the British Library.

Design: Stuart Davies

UK: Printed and bound by CPI Group (UK) Ltd, Croydon, CR0 4YY
US: Printed and bound by Thomson-Shore, 7300 West Joy Road, Dexter, MI 48130

We operate a distinctive and ethical publishing philosophy in
all areas of our business, from our global network of authors to
production and worldwide distribution.

Contents

Welcome to my kitchen...

Cooking is one of my passions in life, more specifically baking. The creating of cakes, cookies and bread is my escape. Food in all its forms is magical. Every single ingredient carries magic with it. Cooking isn't just about feeding; it is about celebrating life and all that Mother Nature offers and sharing it with family and friends.

Practically Pagan - An Alternative Guide to Cooking is designed to take you through the seasons.

Cooking with produce when it is at its best (and cheapest).
Family style cooking to nourish the body, spirit and soul.
Recipes for all, reflecting the energy of each month.

There are 12 sections with recipes for each month to reflect the product that is in season, which include; meat main, vegetarian/ vegan main, soups, standard and vegan desserts, bread and of course...cake; both standard and vegan cake options.

Who am I?

I am a witch ... and have been for a very long time. I am also a working wife and mother who has also been lucky enough to write and have published a book or fifteen. I love to learn, I love to study and have done so from books, online resources, schools and wonderful mentors over the years and continue to learn every day but have learnt the most from getting outside and doing it.

I like to laugh, bake and eat cake...

I am High Priestess of the Kitchen Witch Coven and an Elder at the online Kitchen Witch School.

I also have regular blogs on:

Witches & Pagans - www.witchesandpagans.com/pagan-paths-blogs/hedge-witch.html

Patheos Pagan - www.patheos.com/blogs/beneaththemoon

Moon Books - www.johnhuntpublishing.com/moon-books/

My website and personal blog: www.rachelpatterson.co.uk

Facebook: www.facebook.com/rachelpattersonbooks

Email: kitchenwitchhearth@yahoo.com

Kitchen Witch School website and blog: www.kitchen witchhearth.net

www.facebook.com/kitchenwitchuk

My craft is a combination of old religion Witchcraft, Kitchen Witchery, Hedge Witchery and folk magic. My heart is that of a Kitchen Witch.

My Other Books
Pagan Portals: Kitchen Witchcraft
Grimoire of a Kitchen Witch
Pagan Portals: Hoodoo Folk Magic
Pagan Portals: Moon Magic
A Kitchen Witch's World of Magical Plants & Herbs

A Kitchen Witch's World of Magical Foods
Pagan Portals: Meditation
The Art of Ritual
Arc of the Goddess (co-written with Tracey Roberts)
Pagan Portals: The Cailleach
Moon Books Gods & Goddesses Colouring Book (Patterson family)
Pagan Portals: Animal Magic
Witchcraft ... into the Wilds
Kitchen Witchcraft Series: Spells & Charms
Kitchen Witchcraft Series: Garden Magic
Pagan Portals Sun Magic
Kitchen Witchcraft Series: Crystal Magic

What is Pagan cooking?

I seem to have a bit of a reputation for cake...and I must admit I do love baking. I find it quite therapeutic. When I was asked to write a book proposal for 'pagan cooking' I was, of course, excited about the prospect, but then it got me to thinking, what exactly is 'pagan cooking'?

Over the past few years I have had the pleasure of writing a Kitchen Witchcraft column for Pagan Dawn magazine and in it I have covered food for sabbats, different intents (such as prosperity, love, etc) and food to honour particular deities.

Is this perhaps what I would call 'pagan cooking'?

If it is, then is that a bit restrictive?

What does it cover?

In my ponderings I have come to the conclusion that it covers quite a lot...

Cooking specific foods and dishes for the sabbats.

Using magical ingredients that correspond to particular intents, such as love and prosperity.

Creating food dishes to honour deity.

Baking bread and cookies to consume within ritual.

Food prepared to serve at workshops and gatherings.

Dishes created in harmony with the moon phase.

Working with seasonal ingredients.

Being mindful of where your ingredients are sourced from.

I could probably go on to include pretty much everything including cooking food for your family. Which I do on a daily basis and it always involves using seasonal ingredients and being mindful of where the ingredients are sourced from.

Whenever I cook, I add a dash of magic, whether it is cakes for an open ritual or dinner for my family. I recognise and acknowledge the energy of each ingredient. I stir clockwise to bring positive energy in. When I wash the vegetables, I visualise negative energy draining away, and I try not to cook if I am in a grumpy mood. (Your energy will affect the success of the meal and transfer to the ingredients).

The key

For me, the key point is probably seasonal. I believe we have gotten incredibly lost in the world of food supplies. Being able to purchase strawberries in December is convenient but they never taste of anything because they are grown out of season, often in a polytunnel somewhere around the globe. Not to mention the cost of airfare to ship them here and the eco damage incurred as a result.

When I was a child my father always had an allotment for growing fruit and vegetables, in fact he still does grow a lot of his own produce. In the past I owned my own allotment, but I sadly don't have the time to give it the attention it would need these days. I do have a small garden where I grow lots of herbs and plants and last year acquired a greenhouse too, so I do my bit in a small way.

I have for many years subscribed to local vegetable and fruit box deliveries. Fresh locally grown and sourced produce delivered without any plastic bags or unrecyclable packaging. It is a little bit more expensive than supermarket produce but the quality is far superior, as is the taste. Not only do I get delicious items but there is no waste packaging and I am supporting local growers. Of course, it is all seasonal as well.

Mindful

I do eat meat, although much less than I used to and not every day. However, I am very mindful of where the meat is sourced from. In an ideal world I would also purchase my meat from a local organic supplier, but the price is a bit outside of my budget as I have to feed a family of five, all with healthy appetites. I do make sure the meat I purchase is farm assured and I always buy free range eggs. At least I know that the animals have been well cared for. Having worked on a farm in my younger days I am well aware of the 'other side' of the fence from a farming point of view.

Supermarkets are very convenient, and they do sell cheaper items, but there is a knock-on effect. If the supermarket wants to sell meat or produce at a cheap price then they will force the suppliers and farmers down in price, which puts a lot of strain on them to produce in quantity at stupidly cheap prices.

Farmers markets are excellent if you have one near you and do support your local shops if you can. Sadly, there are no local greengrocers in my area but the lovely veggie box people deliver which makes life much easier.

Little waste

Back to my childhood again, when food didn't seem to ever be wasted. Sunday we had a roast dinner, if it was beef then on Monday we had baked potatoes with cold beef and on Tuesday we had rissoles made with the last of the beef minced up and mixed with the left-over potato. One joint of meat served four of us for three days. Bubble and squeak was a regular too, using up any cooked vegetables and potatoes. One of my favourite cakes is bread pudding, a recipe created to use stale bread and of course treacle tart which uses stale breadcrumbs. Bananas that are particularly ripe get made into banana cake. I often make a big chilli on a Sunday and on the Monday we have the remainder served over baked potatoes or on top of hot dogs. Any vegetables at the end of the week, just before my next vegetable box delivery, get thrown into a stock pot and made into soup. The amount of food that is thrown away in the world each day is shocking. Just a bit of creative thinking makes food go a long way. It will reduce food waste and help the environment, but also help your pocket too.

I have waffled on and probably gone a little astray, but I think this is all part of what 'pagan cooking' means to me. I am a Pagan Witch, I cook every day - so I always work with pagan cooking!

Convenience

I know I have pushed buying fresh produce locally and using what is in season. However, I am also totally realistic. I am a working wife and mother to hungry (and expensive) teenage children. Cooking should be enjoyable, but I do know that having to create a meal every day for the family can sometimes be a chore. I put my hands up to it - I often use frozen vegetables and tinned fruit...there you go, my secret is out. It is OK, honestly the food police are not going to bash down your door if you make soup from a couple of bags of frozen veg. Or if you make a pie using tinned fruit. In fact, I have made some brilliant dishes using frozen produce. Some vegetables I find are better frozen. Peas for example, shelling a bucket load of peas to get enough for a family meal would take hours and I don't have that kind of time. Frozen peas are an excellent ingredient. French beans are also good frozen. I find broccoli, carrots and cauliflower go a bit mushy to serve from frozen as a side dish, but they work brilliantly in soups and casseroles. Sweet potato and butternut squash from the freezer work really well for mash, casserole and soups. The only vegetable I don't ever buy frozen is Brussels sprouts. I love sprouts, but frozen ones are just so mushy and tasteless. I often keep frozen berries in the freezer, they make good crumbles and pies, but the fruit does go very squishy when defrosted. Do what works for you and makes things easier, life is complicated enough as it is!

Foraging

I haven't included wild ingredients because that would be a whole book in itself and I do believe it needs very careful instructions. Mother Nature provides us with a whole host of edible wild plants, but you really need to make perfectly sure that you have identified the plant correctly. Mother Nature also provides a whole host of plants that are poisonous. It is an interesting area however, if you are taken by it, do your homework, research properly, find a local guide and/or course and make sure your knowledge is good before you eat anything.

Across the globe

I love food from all kinds of cuisine (although to be honest I am not really taken with sushi; I need to be convinced about that one). As a family we eat a lot of traditional British dishes but also love Indian and Mexican cooking in particular. I love to experiment, and I am always excited to taste new dishes and ingredients. This book contains a lot of our family favourites and they are a mixture of flavours and regions. If you don't like a particular ingredient in one of the recipes, swap it out for something you do like. I have tried to include common ingredients that are easily obtainable but if you can't get hold of something in your area/country do a quick Google search for substitutes. Part of the fun of cooking is experimenting and making a dish your own.

Herbs

I haven't included herbs in the seasonal list because a lot of people do tend to use dried herbs which, obviously, we have to hand all year around. However, if you grow your own or want to buy fresh then there are some that can be picked pretty much all year round such as sage, thyme, bay and rosemary. Others are the softer leaf herbs which are better in the summer like basil, mint, oregano, tarragon and parsley.

Variations

I have tried to include variations or options for most of the recipes. If you have a household with a mixture of meat eaters and vegetarians or vegans it can get quite complicated making a meal. The options I have included will hopefully help to make life a bit simpler, at least on the cooking front. By taking one main meal, for example, and adding in or taking out the meat element. Other recipes include options to change the flavours or make different versions. There is also a section at the end of the book that gives gluten free and vegan substitutions. With a few vegan friends, I have recently been experimenting a lot with vegan baking. Even if you are not vegan, do give the recipes a try. I have been extremely pleased with the results and with a lot of the recipes I actually prefer to use the vegan version now as it tastes so good.

Note: Most of the recipes here are designed to serve four people with big healthy appetites, apart from the cakes which will obviously serve more - or four people several times!

January

Bubble and squeak soup
Our Household chilli
Veggie chilli
Refried beans
Red beans and rice
Cornbread muffins
Roti
Breadsticks
Florentine rice tart
Chocolate orange brownies
Sweet potato brownies
Oatmeal raisin cookies
Pasta flora
Orange and cinnamon cupcakes
Luscious hot chocolate

To be honest January never used to be my favourite month. The festivities and exciting energy of December is all over. The weather is cold and dreary, and no one has any money. It feels a bit flat and disappointing. However, it is also the start of a new calendar year, the chance to put new things into action. The weather is cold in January in the UK so for me it is still all about comfort food. Eating lettuce in January seems wrong and it isn't in season anyway, bring on the big bowls of steaming hot food and gut busting puddings...

This is a basic list of produce that is usually in season during the month of January. It will obviously vary depending on where you are in the world and what the weather has been like. Be guided by what you find in your local greengrocers or farmers market. If you shop in the supermarket, check for labels that say it is 'new season'.

Beetroot, Brussels sprouts, Cabbage (green/white/red), carrots, celeriac, celery, leeks, onions, parsnips, potatoes, radish, spinach, swede, greens, turnips.

Apples, pears, forced rhubarb (UK).

Grapefruit, lemons, oranges, tangerines (USA).

Bubble and squeak soup

Bubble and squeak is a staple in the UK, often seen on dinner tables on a Monday to use up the left-over vegetables and potatoes from the roast dinner on Sunday. The name comes from the noise that the veggies make when they are frying in the pan! This takes the ingredients and puts them into a soup.

Ingredients
1 tablespoon olive oil
1 chopped onion
500g/1 lb potatoes, diced (I don't peel them, but you can if you prefer)
250g/9 oz carrots, peeled and diced
1.5 litres/3 pints vegetable stock (or chicken if you prefer)
500g/1 lb Brussels sprouts, finely sliced
2 teaspoons dried parsley
Handful of grated cheese (optional)
Salt and pepper

Method
Heat the oil in the pan and sauté the onion for about five minutes, until they are soft. Add the potatoes and the carrots and cook over a low heat for a further ten minutes. Pour in the stock, it should come about an inch above the vegetables in the pan. Simmer for another ten minutes. Add in the Brussels sprouts and cook for a further ten minutes, until all the vegetables are tender. Blend in a food processor or with a liquidiser. Reheat, season with salt and pepper and sprinkle with the grated cheese if using.

Options
I have used Brussel sprouts here, but you can substitute them for cabbage or spring greens.

The carrots can be replaced with swede, parsnip or turnip.
The cheese is an optional extra, you could use vegan cheese or leave it out completely.
If you don't like olive oil, then vegetable or coconut oil is absolutely fine.

Our household chilli

We love chilli, it is our usual family Sunday dinner with all the fixings, tortilla chips, guacamole, salsa and sour cream. Oh, and grated cheese, plenty of grated cheese on top! Sometimes I make double the amount and we have it on baked potatoes or hot dogs the next day. Our secret ingredient is stirring the refried beans into the chilli as you cook it. It boosts the flavour enormously.

Ingredients
750g/ 1 ½ lbs beef mince
1 large onion, diced
3 bell peppers, diced (any colour)
2 large carrots, diced
2 cloves garlic, crushed
1 tin (435g) refried beans
2 beef stock cubes
400ml/ 14 fl oz water
1 tablespoon dried basil
2 tablespoons dried oregano
1 heaped tablespoon cocoa powder
2 tablespoons plain (all purpose) flour
1 teaspoon chilli powder
1 tablespoon cumin seeds
Salt & pepper

Method
Pre-heat the oven to 180C/350F/Gas 4.

Brown the mince in a large pan (no need for any oil). Add in the diced onions, garlic, peppers and carrots. Pop the basil, oregano, chilli powder and cumin seeds in too. Simmer for five minutes. Then stir in the tin of refried beans, the cocoa powder, the stock cubes and the flour. Pour in the water. Stir the whole lot together and season with salt and pepper. If it looks a bit dry add a dash more water, remember it will thicken up as it cooks.

Put a lid on the pan and pop it in the oven. It will be ready in about an hour but if you have the time, leave it for two hours as it gets better.

Veggie chilli

You could use the main chilli recipe above and substitute the mince for soya mince or the equivalent weight in diced vegetables. I often make a veggie version using the same recipe. But if you want to mix things up a little, here is a vegetarian chilli option to try.

Ingredients
4 large carrots, peeled and diced
3 bell peppers, diced
1 large courgette (zucchini), diced
2 tablespoons vegetable or olive oil
Salt and pepper
2 onions, diced
2 garlic cloves, crushed
1 or 3 red chillies, finely chopped
2 teaspoons coriander
1 tablespoon tomato puree
250ml/9 fl oz vegetable stock
2 teaspoons soy sauce
2 tins chopped tomatoes (400g x 2)
1 tin baked beans (400g)
1 tin kidney beans (400g)
1 teaspoon sugar
1 tablespoon cocoa powder
½ to 1 teaspoon chilli powder
1 tablespoon cumin seeds
1 teaspoon paprika
1 tablespoon oregano
1 bay leaf

Method

Heat the vegetable oil in a large pan and sauté the onions, garlic and chillies for five minutes. Add the peppers, carrots and courgettes. Then mix in all the spices, cocoa powder, sugar, herbs and season. Stir in the tomato puree and add the stock and soy sauce. Simmer for ten minutes. Tip in the chopped tomatoes, baked beans and kidney beans.

You can then leave this on a low heat on the stove top with a lid on for about half an hour or pop it in a pre-heated oven (180C/350F/Gas 4) for a couple of hours. If it looks dry at any point add a dash of water.

Refried beans

These are a family favourite, we have them with lots of dishes and also use them stirred into chilli recipes.

Ingredients
1 tablespoon olive oil
½ a small onion, finely chopped
¼ teaspoon salt
2 cloves garlic, minced
½ teaspoon chilli powder
¼ teaspoon ground cumin
2 cans pinto, cannelloni or black beans, rinsed and drained
125ml/4.3 fl oz water
2 tablespoons chopped fresh coriander leaf
1 tablespoon lime juice

Method
Warm the olive oil in a pan over a medium heat. Add the onions and the salt. Cook, stirring occasionally until the onions have softened (about 5-8 minutes). Add the garlic, chilli powder and cumin. Cook, stirring continuously for about half a minute then add the drained beans and the water. Stir, then cover and cook for five minutes.

Mash the beans with a fork or potato masher until at least half the beans are fully mashed. How chunky or smooth you make it is up to you. Continue to cook uncovered in the pan for a couple more minutes, stirring continuously.

Remove from the heat then stir in the coriander leaf and the lime juice. Taste and add more seasoning and lime juice if needed.

Red beans and rice

This is a soul food classic, I apologise for my British variation!

Ingredients
1 tin kidney beans
350g/12 ¼ oz long grain rice
2 cloves garlic, minced
1 red or green bell pepper, diced
1 onion, diced
1 teaspoon dried parsley
½ to 1 teaspoon Tabasco sauce (to taste)
Salt and pepper
1 tablespoon vegetable oil

Method
Put the rice in a saucepan with double the amount of water, bring
to the boil then simmer for about 10 minutes until cooked.
In a pan heat the vegetable oil then add the onions, bell pepper,
parsley, Tabasco and garlic. Sauté for about five minutes until
soft then season with salt and pepper. Once cooked give the
kidney beans a light mash with a fork.
Pop the cooked rice into a serving dish and spoon the kidney
bean mixture on top.

Option
I have kept this version vegetarian, but you could add in some
chopped bacon when you fry the onions.

Cornbread muffins

Our house is a bit divided about these, they are somewhere between a savoury muffin and cake. You will either love or hate them. Personally, I think they pair with chilli perfectly.

Ingredients
150g/5 ¼ oz plain (all purpose) flour
150g/5 ¼ oz fine polenta or cornmeal
2 teaspoons baking powder
1 teaspoon salt
Pinch of sugar
250ml/9fl oz buttermilk
1 beaten egg
60ml/2 fl oz vegetable oil
1 jalapeno, sliced - optional

Method
Preheat the oven to 220C/425F/Gas 7.

Mix together the flour, polenta (or cornmeal), baking powder, salt and sugar. Stir in the buttermilk, egg and oil and mix until well combined.

Pour the batter into a greased (or paper cases) 12-hole muffin tin. If you are using chillies sprinkle them over the top of the muffins.

Bake for 20 minutes or until well risen and golden brown.

Note: If you don't have buttermilk you can make your own; add two tablespoons lemon juice to 250ml/9 fl oz of milk and leave it to stand for ten minutes.

Roti

Perfect fluffy flat breads to eat with soup, chilli, stew or curry.

Ingredients
225g/8oz plain flour (all-purpose flour)
1 tablespoon baking powder
1 teaspoon vegetable oil, plus extra for cooking
160ml/5.6 fl oz water

Method
Pop the flour and baking powder into a bowl, gradually add the water mixing into a soft dough. You don't need to knead the dough just bring it together into a soft ball. Pour over the 1 teaspoon of vegetable oil and cover the bowl with clingfilm, rest for 30 minutes.

Roll the dough into a sausage shape and cut into eight equal slices, then roll each piece out into flat circles. You shouldn't need any flour to roll as the oil stops it from sticking to the board or rolling pin.

If you have a non-stick frying pan you won't need any oil to cook these, otherwise heat a dash of oil in a pan over a medium heat. Add the roti one at a time and cook for about 30 seconds, turning a couple of times.

Remove from the heat and keep warm ready to serve.

Breadsticks

These are a bit fiddly to roll out but good to pop on the table to munch whilst you chat and clink glasses before dinner is ready.

Ingredients
250g/9 oz strong white flour
½ teaspoon salt
3g fast action dried yeast (a scant teaspoon)
2 tablespoons olive oil
1 teaspoon dried oregano
150ml/5 fl oz water

Method
Put the flour, salt, yeast and olive oil into a bowl and mix together. Gradually add the water and mix until it comes together as a dough. Pop onto a floured surface and knead for about five minutes. Pop the dough back into the bowl, cover and leave to rest for half an hour.

Preheat the oven to 220C/425F/Gas 7. Line two baking trays with parchment. Pinch off small pieces of the dough (around 15g/½ oz) and roll each one out under the palm of your hand into thin strips (about 25cm/10″) in length. This is tricky and mine usually come out a little uneven but that just adds to the charm…

If you want to, at this stage you can roll the sticks in poppy or sesame seeds.

Place the sticks on the baking trays and bake for about 20 minutes until golden brown.

Options
You can use any herb you want in these, replace the oregano with thyme, parsley, rosemary or chilli flakes also work well too.

Florentine rice tart

I am a bit of a 'proper old-fashioned pudding' kinda gal. Rice pudding is one of my favourites, but this takes it to another level and makes it quite fancy too.

Ingredients

Short crust pastry:
125g/4 ½ oz butter
100g/3 ½ oz icing sugar (powdered sugar)
Small pinch salt
250g/9 oz plain (all purpose) flour
2 large eggs
2 tablespoons cold water or milk

Filling:
55g/2 oz butter
2 teaspoons vanilla extract
325g/11 ½ oz risotto rice
3 tablespoons sugar
1 wineglass of white wine (or water)
1 litre/35 fl oz milk
2 large eggs, whisked
2 tablespoons icing sugar (powdered sugar)

Method

Great a 28cm/11cm loose bottomed tart tin with butter.

To make the pastry cream together the butter, icing sugar and salt then rub in the flour and egg yolks. When the mixture looks like coarse breadcrumbs add the cold milk or water. Pat and gently work the mixture together until you have a ball of dough (don't work the pastry too much). Wrap in clingfilm and pop in the fridge for an hour. Remove after an hour, roll out and line your tart tin. Place in the freezer for an hour.

Preheat the oven to 180C/350F/Gas 4 and bake the pastry case for about 12 minutes or until lightly golden. Remove from the oven and turn the heat up to 200C/400F/Gas 6.

In a large saucepan melt the butter and then add the vanilla extract. Add the rice and sugar. Stir to coat with the butter then add the wine (or water), keep stirring over a medium heat until the liquid has almost cooked away. Now add in the milk bit by bit, keep the rice on a slow simmer for about 15 minutes stirring often. You want the rice to still have a bit of a bite, but you also want it to still have some liquid. Allow the rice mixture to cool slightly then mix in the whisked eggs. Pour the rice into your tart case, sprinkle with icing sugar and bake for about 20-25 minutes until the pastry is golden.

Chocolate orange brownies

Everyone loves a good brownie, and these have the added zing of orange to brighten up even the darkest month.

Ingredients
200g/7 oz butter

75g/2 ½ oz dark chocolate

2 large eggs

225g/8 oz sugar

75g/ 2 ½ oz self-raising flour

2 teaspoons vanilla extract

100g/3 ½ oz chocolate chips

100g/3 ½ oz marmalade

Method
Preheat the oven to 350F/180C/Gas 4.

Grease and line a baking tin.

Chop the butter and dark chocolate into pieces and melt in the microwave for 1 minute, stir then repeat until both are melted.

Gently fold in the rest of the ingredients. Tip into the prepared baking tin and smooth the top.

Bake for 25-30 minutes. The middle of the brownie will wobble slightly, the mixture continues to set once out of the oven.

Allow to cool in the tin.

Options
Replace the chocolate chips with chopped nuts.

Substitute the orange marmalade for lime marmalade, lemon curd or raspberry jam.

For a different flavour add peanut butter instead of marmalade.

Use white chocolate chips.

Sweet potato brownies (vegan)

I love sweet potatoes and they work brilliantly in a brownie recipe to create a vegan/dairy free treat.

Ingredients
250g/9 oz peanut or almond butter
150g/5 ¼ oz sweet potato puree
2 teaspoons vanilla extract
50g/1 ¾ oz self-raising flour
130g/4 ½ oz sugar
40g/1 ½ oz cocoa powder
3 teaspoons baking powder
½ teaspoon mixed spice
85g/3 oz chocolate chips

Method
Preheat your oven to 350F/180C/Gas 4.

Grease and line a brownie tin.

Gently heat the nut butter until it is soft.

Whisk the nut butter into the potato puree and add the vanilla.

In a separate bowl mix together the flour, sugar, cocoa, baking powder and spice.

Pour the wet ingredients into the dry and fold until combined. Stir in the chocolate chips.

Bake for 20 minutes. The centre of the brownie will still wobble, but it sets more as it cools.

Oatmeal raisin cookies (vegan option)

These are a real comfort, feel good kind of cookie. The ones you want to eat when you are in for the night, on the sofa with a blanket and a mug of hot chocolate watching old movies.

Ingredients
185g/6 ½ oz plain flour (all-purpose flour)
225g/8 oz porridge oats
150g/5 ¼ oz raisins or sultanas
1 ½ teaspoons mixed spice
½ teaspoon bicarbonate soda
½ teaspoon salt
150g/5 ¼ oz margarine (or vegan margarine)
150g/5 ¼ oz brown sugar
50g/1 ¾ oz sugar
2 teaspoons vanilla extract
1 tablespoon water

Method

Preheat your oven to 350F/180C/Gas 4. Line two baking sheets with baking parchment.

Whisk the margarine, both sugars, vanilla and water until combined.

In a separate bowl mix together the flour, spice, bicarbonate soda and salt then gently stir this into the margarine mixture. Then fold in the oats and the raisins.

Pop scoops of the mixture onto the baking sheets, leaving space for them to spread. You should get about 28 cookies from this mixture.

Bake for 12-14 minutes, until the edges are golden.

Options

I prefer to use sultanas instead of raisins, they are sweeter and more plumptious.

Replace the raisins with chopped dried apricots, cranberries or dried cherries.

Substitute the raisins for chopped nuts or chocolate chips.

Pasta flora (Greek jam tart)

Forget the jam tarts you used to get for school dinners or in packets, this is a very grown up dessert worthy of any dinner table. I have used shop bought pastry and jam for this because it makes it so simple, but you can of course make your own. (Pastry recipe included in 'The Basics' section at the end of the book).

Ingredients
One packet readymade sweet shortcrust pastry
One jar raspberry (or your favourite flavour) jam
Butter for greasing
Milk or egg for glazing

Method
Grease a pie dish with butter. Roll out the pastry and line the bottom of the pie dish. Spread the jam over the base. Roll out the remaining dough and cut into strips. Create a lattice pattern for the top of the tart, lay it over the bottom. You may need to wet the pastry edges with a little water to help the pastry stick together.

Brush the top with milk or beaten egg.

Bake in a preheated oven at 350F/180C/Gas 4 for 30-40 minutes. Serve cool.

Orange and cinnamon cupcakes

Can't stop eating these...

Ingredients

Cakes:
190g/6 ½ oz butter, softened
190g/6 ½ oz caster sugar
190g/6 ½ oz self-raising flour
3 large eggs
Grated zest of 4 oranges

Icing:
300ml/10 ½ fl oz double (heavy) cream
200g/7 oz mascarpone cream
1 teaspoon ground cinnamon
2 tablespoons caster sugar

Method

Preheat the oven to 180C/350F/Gas Mk 4.

Grease a 12-hole muffin tin with butter.

Pop all the cake ingredients into a large bowl and whisk together until light and creamy (yup it's that easy). Divide the mixture between the 12 muffin holes. Bake for about 20 minutes. Leave them in the tin for about 5-10 minutes then turn them out onto a rack to cool completely.

To make the icing whisk the mascarpone and cream together with the sugar and cinnamon until it forms stiff peaks.

Cut each cake in half and pipe or spread the icing on the cut half and press the two halves together. I like to turn the cakes upside down as it looks better but go with what works for you. Then pipe a pretty swirl of icing on the top.

Luscious hot chocolate

This is a totally lush hot chocolate mix, make up larger quantities and keep the powder mix in a jar.

Ingredients
2 tablespoons Horlicks (malted milk drink)
2 tablespoons cornflour (corn starch)
3 tablespoons icing sugar (powdered sugar)
4 tablespoons cocoa powder
100g/3 ½ oz dark chocolate, finely grated
1 pinch ground cinnamon
1 pinch sea salt

Method
For an individual mug of hot chocolate with half a pint of milk use 5 heaped teaspoons of the mixture.

Pour the milk into a saucepan and bring almost to the boil then spoon the chocolate mix into the hot milk, give it a whisk and leave to simmer in the saucepan for a couple of minutes before serving - it will come together as a nice thick gloopy consistency.

Serve as is or top with whipped cream, marshmallows and a couple of Maltesers or a sprinkling of grated chocolate.

Options
Ring the changes by using milk or white chocolate in the mixture instead of dark chocolate, you could even use grated Caramac for a caramel flavour drink.

February

Parsnip and celeriac soup
Pulled pork
Chickpea stew
Colcannon
Cumin and fennel loaf
Boxty bread
Sticky toffee pudding
Love cake
Depression cake
Double chocolate cookies
Magic custard cake
Chocolate and spice cookies
Cinnamon or chocolate buns
Peanut butter hot chocolate

February is a month of promises. January is done with and March is on the horizon. Spring isn't here yet, and often not even any sign of it, but that hint is in the air. February is still all about warming comfort food, but it also includes Imbolc at the beginning of the month. This is the Pagan festival of light to celebrate the coming of spring with new beginnings, purification and renewal. It is a time of potential, ideas and fertility. Animals are giving birth to their new offspring or are just about to, so milk and dairy products are often key ingredients in Imbolc celebrations. But any kind of fresh and light vegetables as well as lots of herbs and spices are used.

This is a basic list of produce that is usually in season during the month of February. It will obviously vary depending on where you are in the world and what the weather has been like. Be guided by what you find in your local greengrocers or farmers market. If you shop in the supermarket, check for labels that say it is 'new season'.

Beetroot, Brussels sprouts, cabbages (green/white/red), carrots, celeriac, celery, chives, leeks, onions, parsnips, potatoes, radish, spinach, swede, greens.

Apples, forced rhubarb (UK).

Grapefruit, lemons, oranges (USA).

Parsnip and celeriac soup

Celeriac has a real celery taste, you will either love it or hate it, but I think it pairs really well with parsnip (another love or hate vegetable!). Definitely a warming feel-good soup.

Ingredients
1 litre/35 fl oz vegetable stock
4 parsnips, peeled and diced
1 onion, chopped
½ celeriac root, peeled and diced
2 cloves garlic, peeled and crushed
½ teaspoon fennel seeds
Salt and pepper

Method
This is so easy - literally throw everything into the pan together; veggies, stock and seasoning. Bring to the boil then lower the heat and simmer for about half an hour to forty minutes, until the vegetables are tender.
Blitz the soup in a food processor or liquidiser (or mash by hand if you are feeling really strong...and patient).
Reheat and serve.

Options
Replace the celeriac with a whole fennel bulb, diced.
Use cumin seeds instead of fennel for a warmer spicy taste.
If you really hate celeriac or fennel use 2 large carrots instead.

Pulled pork

This is an easy dish that you can make and just leave in the oven. It works well served with mashed potato or fries. We like to use the left overs in baguettes to make a very messy sandwich.

Ingredients
A shoulder of pork
400ml/14 fl oz stock (vegetable or chicken)
A medium size piece of root ginger (about 2 inches long) sliced
4 star anise
Freshly ground black pepper
4 cloves of garlic, sliced

Method
Set the oven on low (around Gas 2/150C/350F).

Place the piece of pork fat side up in a roasting tin, pour the stock and add all the other ingredients into the tin as well.

Cover the tin loosely with tin foil.

Pop in the oven and leave it for a good 4 to 5 hours then test it to see how it is getting on (depending on the size of the joint it may take longer). If the meat comes away from the bone with a fork then it is ready, if not take the tin foil off and leave for another hour.

This dish is very forgiving, if left covered with the foil you can leave it in the oven all day (just keep an eye on it).

Once the meat is ready you can take it all from the bone - 'pulling' it with a fork or with your fingers. This can then be put in a roasting dish.

Strain the juices from the tin into a jug and pour the stock over the pulled meat - this keeps it moist. You can cover this with foil and leave in the oven to keep warm until you are ready for it.

Chickpea stew

This stew has a touch of Moroccan flavouring to it. Simple to make and delicious to eat.

Ingredients
1 tin chickpeas (400g)
2 bell peppers, diced
2 teaspoon ground coriander
2 tablespoon tomato puree
2 onions, sliced
1 teaspoon chilli flakes
2 teaspoons ground cumin
2 large courgettes (zucchini), diced
2 large carrots, peeled and diced
2 tablespoons vegetable or olive oil
500ml/1-pint vegetable stock

Method
Heat the oil in a large pan and add the onion, sauté for five minutes. Add the courgette, carrots and peppers, cook for another five minutes.

Add in the coriander, cumin, chilli flakes and tomato puree, then pour in the stock.

Simmer for about twenty minutes then add in the chickpeas. Cook for a further five minutes.

Options
Sprinkle chopped almonds over the top and a spoonful of plain yoghurt.

Substitute the courgettes for aubergine - this is more traditional, but I don't like aubergine!

Colcannon

A nod to the Celts, this is lovely eaten on its own but also works well served with crispy bacon or sausages.

Ingredients
1kg/2.2 lbs potatoes, well-scrubbed (cut any large ones in half)
100g/3 ½ oz butter
Half a small green cabbage, finely shredded
150ml/5 fl oz double cream (full fat milk, soya cream or almond milk also work well)

Method
Tip the potatoes into a large saucepan of water. Bring to the boil, then simmer for 15-20 mins, or until the flesh is tender when pierced.

Meanwhile, heat a quarter of the butter in a saucepan, then fry the bacon (if using) and the cabbage for 5 minutes. Turn off the heat and set aside. Drain potatoes in a colander.

Mash potato until smooth. Heat cream with remaining butter and, when almost boiling, beat into the potato.

Add cabbage to potato and mix. Season with salt and pepper.

Cumin and fennel loaf

This bread tastes amazing and definitely something to warm your heart on a cold February day, or any day of the year really.

Ingredients
500g/1 lb strong white bread flour
1 teaspoon salt
2 teaspoons cumin seeds
1 teaspoon fennel seeds
1 ½ teaspoon dried easy blend yeast
350ml/12 fl oz lukewarm water

Method
Mix the flour, salt, cumin and fennel seeds together. Add the dried yeast and mix. Gradually add the water and mix together to form a soft dough. Knead in a mixer for five minutes or by hand for ten minutes. If you are kneading by hand use a splosh of olive oil on your surface rather than adding more flour, this will help the dough not to stick. Knead until your dough is soft and springy.

Pop the dough in an oiled bowl and cover with a tea towel. Leave in a warm place for about an hour, until the dough has doubled in size.

Turn the dough out and knead it gently for about a minute, then shape into a round and place on a baking sheet lined with baking parchment. Cover again and leave to rise until doubled, about 45 minutes.

Pre heat the oven to 220C/425F/Gas 7.

Spray the top of the dough with water then sprinkle with a pinch of flour. Pop into the oven and bake for 15 minutes. Then reduce the oven to 190C/375F/Gas 5 and bake for a further half an hour. Until the loaf is a nice golden brown and sounds hollow when tapped underneath.

Boxty bread

This is a traditional Irish festival bread, flat and round and marked into four portions before baking. It was often eaten on Shrove Tuesday, All Saints Day and Halloween.

Ingredients
225g/8 oz raw potatoes
225g/8 oz mashed potatoes
225g/8 oz plain flour (all-purpose flour)
50g/1 ¾ oz butter, melted
Salt & pepper

Method
Preheat the oven to 190C/375F/gas mark 5. Grease a baking tray.

Wash and peel the raw potatoes then grate them into a clean cloth (tea towel) and wring them well over a bowl to squeeze out the juice. Place the grated potatoes in a bowl together with the mashed potatoes and mix.

Leave the starchy liquid in the bowl until the starch has settled then pour off the liquid and add the starch to the potatoes. Add the flour, melted butter and seasoning and mix to a soft dough. Knead well. Divide into two portions (this mixture makes two loaves) and roll into flat rounds (you may need to flour the board). Place on the baking tray and divide the top of each loaf into four with a sharp knife. Bake for 40 minutes until firm and golden. Remove from the oven and serve warm with butter.

Sticky toffee pudding

If we had to choose just one dessert for our family, this would be it. This recipe makes for a very happy husband...

Ingredients
160g/5 ½ oz whole dates, stoned and roughly chopped (or put in a blender)
150ml/5 fl oz boiling water
1 teaspoon vanilla extract
90g/3 oz butter, softened, plus extra for greasing
150g/5 ¼ oz light muscovado sugar
2 large free-range eggs
2 tablespoons golden syrup
175g/6 oz self-raising flour
1 teaspoon bicarbonate of soda
100ml/3 ½ fl oz whole milk

For the toffee sauce:
225g/8 oz light muscovado sugar
100g/3 ½ oz unsalted butter, softened
275ml/9 ½ fl oz double cream
1 tablespoon golden syrup

Method
Put the dates in a mixing bowl with the water. Leave for 30 minutes until cool, then mash with a fork to a rough pulp or blitz in a blender. I blitz them because we prefer a pudding without lumps of date. Stir through the vanilla and set aside.
Butter a 1.2 litre ovenproof dish and set aside. Heat the oven to 170C/325F/gas 3.
While the dates are soaking, use an electric mixer or wooden spoon to beat the 90g/3 oz butter and 150g/5 ¼ oz sugar until light and creamy.

Add the eggs one at a time, beating well before adding the next. Beat in the syrup, then mix the flour with the bicarbonate of soda and gently fold in one third using a metal spoon.

Fold in a third of the milk, then repeat until all the flour and milk are used up. Stir the soaked dates, with their liquid, into the batter - it may curdle, but don't worry. Spoon into the prepared dish.

Bake for 50 minutes or until the pudding is risen and firm, and a skewer pushed into the middle comes out clean (cover with foil after 40 minutes if the edges are browning too much).

Meanwhile, make the toffee sauce. Put the 225g/8 oz sugar, 100g/3 ½ oz butter and HALF the cream in a large, heavy-based pan and heat gently.

When the sugar has dissolved, turn up the heat, stir in the syrup and bubble, stirring, for 2-3 minutes until the mix is a rich toffee colour. Take the pan off the heat and stir in the rest of the cream. Keep warm.

Leave the pudding to cool for 20 minutes, then skewer it all over and pour over half the sauce. Leave for another 15 minutes, then serve drizzled with the rest of the sauce.

Love cake

With February having the flavour of love this cake totally fits the bill.

Ingredients
125g/4 ½ oz butter, room temperature

325g/11 ½ oz sugar

6 eggs

200g/7 oz fine semolina

100g/3 ½ oz ground cashews (or ground almonds)

5 ½ tablespoons honey

2 teaspoons ground cinnamon

½ teaspoon grated nutmeg

1 teaspoon ground cardamom (or finely ground seeds of 12 pods)

1 teaspoon vanilla essence

Zest of 1 lemon

Zest of 1 orange

Method
Preheat the oven to 150C/300F/Gas 2. Line a rectangular cake tin (approx. 30cm x 20cm) with greaseproof paper and butter.

Cream the butter and sugar together in a bowl and set aside. In another bowl beat the eggs until pale and smooth, then slowly whisk them into the sugar and butter mixture. Fold in the semolina, ground nuts, honey, cinnamon, nutmeg, cardamom, vanilla essence and citrus zest.

Fold the mixture together and spoon into your cake tin. Pop in the oven and bake for 45 minutes or until the top is golden brown and firm to the touch. Leave to cool before cutting or taking out of the cake tin.

Depression cake

I know the name doesn't sound the most inspiring. I promise you won't feel down when you eat it! The name actually comes from the Great Depression when they had to get creative with recipes due to the lack of eggs or dairy. This cake is exceptionally light and fluffy.

Ingredients
450g/15 ¾ oz sugar
450g/15 ¾ oz plain flour (all-purpose flour)
5 heaped tablespoons cocoa powder
2 teaspoons bicarbonate soda
1 teaspoon salt
10 tablespoons vegetable oil
2 teaspoons vanilla extract
2 tablespoons cider vinegar
500ml/1-pint water

Method
Preheat your oven to 350F/180C/Gas 4.
Mix together all the ingredients and pour into an ungreased 9 x 13" baking tin.
Bake for 40 minutes.

Double chocolate cookies (vegan option)

I have made a lot of chocolate cookies in my time and eaten even more. This is one of the best recipes I have ever made. Crunchy on the outside and soft gooey goodness on the inside - perfect.

Ingredients
110g/4 oz margarine (vegan option)
100g/3 ½ oz sugar
100g/3 ½ oz brown sugar
1 teaspoon vanilla extract
125g/ 4 ½ oz plain flour (all-purpose flour)
56g/2 oz cocoa powder
1 teaspoon bicarbonate soda
¼ teaspoon salt
1 tablespoon milk (soya/almond option)
100g/3 ½ oz dark chocolate chips (vegan option)

Method
Preheat your oven to 350F/180C/Gas 4.

Line a baking sheet with baking parchment.

Whisk the margarine and both sugars together until light and fluffy. Add the vanilla.

In a separate bowl mix together the flour, cocoa powder, bicarbonate soda and salt.

Add the dry ingredients to the wet and mix together. It will be crumbly.

Add the tablespoon of milk and bring together to form a dough.

Mix in the chocolate chips.

The mixture will be thick but should be sticky enough to roll into small balls. Pop these onto the prepared baking sheet.

Bake for 10 minutes. The edges will be firm but the centre still soft. They will firm up as they cool.

Magic custard cake

This really is a magic cake, full of gorgeous custardy goodness.

Ingredients
4 eggs (whites separated from yolks), room temp
1 teaspoon vanilla extract
150g/5 ¼ oz sugar
120g/4 ¼ oz butter, melted
100g/3 ½ oz plain flour (all purpose)
500ml/1-pint milk, lukewarm
Icing/powdered sugar for dusting cake

Method
Preheat oven to 170C/325F/Gas 3.

Grease and Line 8 inch x 8 inch baking dish with parchment.

Separate eggs and add the egg whites to a mixer and beat egg whites stiff.

Place egg whites in a bowl and set aside.

Beat the egg yolks & sugar until light. Add butter and vanilla. Beat for two mins.

Add the flour and mix it in until fully incorporated.

Slowly start adding the milk and beat until everything is well mixed together. Add the egg whites, a third at a time and gently fold them in using a spatula, repeat until all egg whites are folded in.

Pour batter into baking dish and bake for approx. 60 minutes or until the top is lightly golden.

Cool and dust heavily with powdered sugar.

Chocolate and spice cookies

I made these for one of our Kitchen Witch open rituals and they went down very well, I almost started to panic in case there weren't enough left to take home for me...

Ingredients
175g/6 oz butter, softened
200g/7 oz dark muscovado sugar
75g/2 ½ oz caster sugar
½ teaspoon ground cinnamon
¼ teaspoon ground cloves
¼ teaspoon ground nutmeg
1 large egg
1 egg yolk
250g/9 oz self-raising flour
175g/6 oz plain chocolate chips (or finely chopped chocolate)
175g/6 oz chopped pistachio or cashew nuts (or a mixture)

Method
Preheat the oven to 180C/350F/Gas Mk 4. Line two baking trays with parchment paper.

Cream together the butter, sugars and spices until light and creamy (this is much easier if you have an electric whisk/ mixer). Mix in the whole egg and the yolk. Then add the flour, chocolate and the chopped nuts. Mix together to form a dough.

Take tablespoonfuls of the dough and pop them on the baking tray evenly spaced with enough room for them to spread. Bake for 12-15 minutes. They should be golden but still chewy in the centre.

Cinnamon or chocolate buns

Half our household loves cinnamon the other half hates it... solution? Make half a batch of cinnamon buns and half a batch of chocolate buns.

Ingredients
125ml/4.3 fl oz milk
175ml/6 fl oz water
40g/1 ½ oz unsalted butter
1 tablespoon honey
7g sachet/2 teaspoons fast acting yeast
450g/15 ¾ oz white strong bread flour
1 teaspoon salt

Filling:
100g/3 ½ oz unsalted butter, melted
100g/3 ½ oz brown/demerara sugar
2 teaspoons ground cinnamon and 100g/3 ½ oz milk chocolate (chopped)

Icing:
125g/4 ½ oz icing sugar (powdered sugar)
1 teaspoon vanilla extract
Water
100g/3 ½ oz milk chocolate

Method
Grease a 12-hole muffin pan with butter and set aside.

Warm the milk, water, honey and butter in a saucepan until the butter just starts to melt and the liquid is lukewarm.

Put the flour, yeast and salt into a mixer with a dough hook.

Pour the lukewarm liquid mix onto the flour and mix with the dough hook for about 5 to 6 minutes. Or knead by hand for about 10 minutes - until the dough is soft and smooth.

Place in an oiled bowl and cover with cling wrap, leave for 90 minutes until dough is doubled in size.

Tip the dough onto a floured work surface and knock back by kneading for 30 seconds.

Roll the dough thinly into a rectangle (about 1cm deep).

If you are making half cinnamon and half chocolate cut the rolled-out dough in half.

Brush all over with the melted butter then sprinkle over the sugar and cinnamon evenly over one half and the sugar and chopped chocolate over the other half.

With the longest edge farthest away from you, use both hands to carefully roll the rectangles towards you keeping the roll tight.

Divide each roll into 6 equal slices (so you have 12 in total). Place the buns into the buttered muffin pan with the cut side uppermost and cover loosely with oiled cling film or a tea towel and leave to rise for half an hour.

Preheat the oven to 190C/375F/Gas 5.

Remove the cling film and bake the buns for 15-20 minutes until well risen and golden brown.

Transfer to a cooling rack and make the icing:

Mix the icing sugar with the vanilla extract and enough water to bring it to a stiff dropping consistency.

Melt the milk chocolate.

Spread the white icing over the cinnamon buns with a palette knife.

Pour the melted chocolate over the chocolate buns and smooth out with a palette knife.

Options

To make these into fruit Chelsea buns add 300g/10 ½ oz of chopped dried mixed fruit.

Peanut butter hot chocolate

Add a peanut hit to your hot chocolate.

Ingredients
710ml/25 ½ fl oz milk
115g/4 oz sugar
25g/0.8 oz cocoa powder
62ml/2 fl oz water
3 tablespoons smooth peanut butter
85g/3 oz grated chocolate
Pinch salt

Method
Pop the sugar and cocoa powder into a saucepan and whisk together until they are smooth then whisk in the milk over a medium heat until the liquid starts to steam.

Remove the pan from the heat and add in the peanut butter and the chocolate, then whisk together. Add a pinch of salt and then top with cream or marshmallows or even a few peanuts if you want to.

March

Leek, potato and sage soup
Creole chicken
Chana and spinach curry
Bombay eggs
Feisty fennel greens
Buckwheat and rye loaf
Pitta bread
Apple pie with cheddar crust
Chocolate mayonnaise cake
Chai cupcakes
Spring cookies
Anise cookies
Greek bougatsa
Red velvet hot chocolate

March is often when we start to see the first signs of spring or if Mother Nature is being fickle (as she so often is) we can also get snow! But it does have the feel that spring isn't too far around the corner. March also hosts the spring equinox, or Ostara as it is often called by modern pagans. Darkness and light are in balance as the earth begins to stir. And of course, this month includes chocolate eggs, which is never a bad thing.

This is a basic list of produce that is usually in season during the month of March. It will obviously vary depending on where you are in the world and what the weather has been like. Be guided by what you find in your local greengrocers or farmers market. If you shop in the supermarket, check for labels that say it is 'new season'.

Brussels sprouts, cabbage (green/white), carrots, cauliflower, celeriac, chives, greens, leeks, mushrooms, onions, parsnips, potatoes, purple sprouting, spinach, swede.

Apples, forced rhubarb (UK).

Pineapples (USA).

Leek, potato and sage soup

This adds a bit of a twist to the usual recognised leek and potato soup; you can keep it veggie or switch it up with added chicken.

Ingredients
50g/1 ¾ oz butter or a dash of vegetable oil
1 onion, chopped
1 tablespoon chopped fresh sage or 1 teaspoon dried sage
450g/15 ¾ oz leeks, finely sliced
450g/15 ¾ oz potatoes, diced (I don't peel them, but you can if you prefer)
1 litre/35 fl oz chicken or vegetable stock
Optional - 250g/9 oz cooked shredded chicken
Salt and pepper

Method
Melt the butter or oil in the pan and add the onion and sage, sauté for about ten minutes. Add the leeks and the potatoes then cover with the stock. Bring to the boil and simmer for about half an hour, until the vegetables are tender.
At this point you can either leave the vegetables chunky or blitz it in a food processor or liquidiser.
Season with salt and pepper.
If you want you can then add in the shredded chicken, reheat and serve.

Options
You can add in the chicken to create a 'roast dinner' soup, you could also add in a handful of chopped fried bacon.
If you don't like sage try replacing it with either parsley or rosemary.
Potatoes can be replaced with either sweet potatoes or squash.

Creole chicken

A bit of sunshine to brighten up your dinner table. Serve with rice.

Ingredients
4 tablespoons vegetable oil
8 chicken pieces
50g/1 ¾ oz plain (all purpose) flour
1 large onion, thinly sliced
1 red bell pepper, diced
1 green bell pepper, diced
3 cloves garlic, crushed
2 chillies, seeded and finely sliced
3 sprigs fresh thyme or 1 teaspoon dried thyme
1 teaspoon dried oregano
2 bay leaves
1 x 400g/14 oz tin chopped tomatoes
350ml/12 fl oz chicken stock
Salt & pepper

Method
Heat the oil in a large casserole dish over a medium heat and sauté the chicken pieces until browned. I prefer to use chicken breast, but you could use legs or thighs. Remove the chicken and set aside, leaving the oils and chicken juices in the pan.

Add the flour into the oil and stir constantly until the flour begins to brown. Add the onion, peppers, garlic and chillies and cook for a few minutes until the vegetables are beginning to soften. Add the thyme, oregano, bay leaves and tomatoes then pour in the stock and stir well.

Return the chicken pieces to the casserole dish cover and simmer for 45 minutes. Taste to season and if the gravy is too thin simmer for a while longer with the lid off, if the gravy is too thick add some water or stock.

This can be made the day before and warmed through to serve.

Options

You can make this vegetarian/vegan by using a butternut squash, cubed or cubed tofu instead of the chicken and replacing the chicken stock with vegetable stock.

Chana and spinach curry

An easy to make and delicious vegetable curry full of 'good for you' spinach.

Ingredients
1 tablespoon vegetable oil
1 onion, finely sliced
2 garlic cloves, crushed
2 chillies, seeded and finely sliced
2 tablespoons curry powder
2 potatoes, diced
400g (14 oz) tin of chickpeas, drained
1 teaspoon tomato ketchup
200g/7 oz shredded spinach
Salt & pepper

Method
Heat the oil in a deep pan over a medium heat. Add the onion, garlic and chillies and cook for about five minutes until soft. Stir in the curry powder and cook for a further five minutes adding in a little more oil or water if needed (to stop it burning).

Stir in the potatoes and chickpeas and season with the tomato ketchup, salt and pepper. Add enough water to just cover and bring to the boil. Then reduce the heat, cover and simmer for 25 minutes until the water has been absorbed. Add the spinach and cook for a further five minutes.

Bombay eggs

A scrummy vegetarian dish.

Ingredients
1 teaspoon cumin seeds
2 teaspoons coriander seeds
4 tablespoons vegetable oil
1 ½ large onions, finely sliced
4 cloves garlic, crushed
3cm root ginger peeled then finely chopped (or grated)
2 tins chopped tomatoes
1 tablespoon tomato puree
1 teaspoon salt
1 teaspoon sugar
½ teaspoon chilli powder
¼ teaspoon ground turmeric
250g/9 oz fresh spinach (or 1 tin of canned spinach)
6 medium eggs
Black pepper

Method
In a large saucepan toast the cumin and coriander seeds over a medium heat for about two minutes, keep them moving... then grind them in a pestle and mortar.

Pour the oil into the pan and pop the spices back in on a medium heat. Add the onions and cook for about five minutes then add the garlic and ginger. Cook for a further two minutes then add in the tomatoes.

Leave to cook and reduce for about 10 minutes, stirring occasionally. Then add in the tomato puree, salt, sugar, chilli powder and turmeric, mix well. Add in the spinach and mix again, if you are using fresh spinach leave to simmer for a couple of minutes for the spinach to wilt.

To bake the eggs, make an egg size well in the tomato sauce then crack an egg into it. Repeat as quickly as you can with the other eggs and put the lid on the pan. Turn the heat down really low and cook for ten minutes or until the whites of the eggs are set.

Finish by sprinkling with fresh black pepper.

Feisty fennel greens

This is in my humble opinion one of the easiest and best ways to serve greens or cabbage and it brings in the feisty fire of fennel.

Ingredients
A cabbage or greens, shredded
Teaspoon of fennel seeds
Tablespoon coconut oil

Method
Heat the oil in a large frying pan or wok over a medium heat then throw in the fennel seeds stirring for a minute then add in the cabbage. Stir fry for a couple of minutes until cooked through and serve.

Buckwheat and rye loaf

A very tasty but incredibly simple to make loaf.

Ingredients
250g/9 oz rye flour
250g/9 oz buckwheat flour
½ teaspoon salt
1 teaspoon fast action dried yeast
1 tablespoon honey
400ml/14 fl oz warm water
1 tablespoon olive oil
Tablespoon sunflower or pumpkin seeds

Method
Mix together the flour, salt and yeast in a large bowl. Dissolve the honey in the warm water and mix into the flour. The mixture will be wet and sticky...don't panic!

Add the oil and seeds and continue to mix for a few minutes then tip into a large loaf tin (1kg). Cover loosely and allow to rise for half an hour.

Preheat the oven to 400F/200C/Gas 6.

Bake for 45 minutes until the top is golden and the bottom makes a hollow sound when you tap it.

Leave to cool before slicing.

Pitta bread

I am a big fan of pitta bread so decided that I would have a go at making my own and I have to say it was *trés simple*, probably one of the easiest bread I have ever made, and the result was scrummy.

Ingredients

250g/9 oz strong white flour, plus extra for dusting

7g sachet/2 teaspoons instant yeast

1 teaspoon salt

160ml/5.6 fl oz water

2 teaspoons olive oil, plus extra for kneading

Method

In a bowl, mix together the flour, yeast and salt.

Add 120ml/4fl oz of the water and the oil.

Using your fingers mix the ingredients together. Gradually add the remaining water and oil until all the flour has come away from the sides and you have a soft dough. (You may not need all the water; the dough should be soft and not sticky.) I actually do this stage and the kneading in my mixer with the bread hook.

Pour a little oil onto your work top. Place the dough on top and knead for 5-10 minutes. The dough will be wet in the beginning but will form a smooth dough once kneaded. Then place your dough in an oiled bowl. Cover and leave to prove until doubled in size.

Preheat the oven to 250C/475F/Gas 9 and place a clean baking tray on the middle shelf.

When the dough has doubled in size, tip it out onto a work surface dusted with flour. Knock the air out of the dough by folding it inwards over and over. Split the dough into 4-6 equally sized balls. Roll each ball into an oval shape 5mm/

¼″ thick.

Remove the hot tray from the oven, dust with flour and place the pitta breads on it. You may have to cook them in batches.

Bake for 5-10 minutes, or until they just start to colour. Remove them from the oven and cover with a clean cloth until they are cool.

Apple pie with cheddar crust

I know it sounds a bit weird but trust me...it works...lush apple filling inside a savoury cheddar pastry...yum!

Ingredients

For the pastry:
75g /2 ½ oz mild cheddar cheese, grated
225g/8 oz plain (all purpose) flour
100g/3 ½ oz butter, softened (if you prefer you can use half lard, half butter)

For the filling:
1kg/2 lbs apples - this can be all eaters or half eaters and half cooking apples
1 level tablespoon fine semolina
75g/2 ½ oz sugar
½ teaspoon ground cloves
½ teaspoon ground cinnamon
1 large egg, beaten - to glaze

Method
First make the pastry. Put the flour into a large bowl then add the butter and lard (if using) cut into small pieces, rubbing the fat into the flour with your fingertips until it reaches the crumbly stage.

Now add the grated Cheddar and enough cold water to make a soft dough that leaves the bowl clean (about 3 tablespoons). Then turn it out on to a board, knead it briefly and lightly, then wrap it in clingfilm and leave it to rest in the fridge for about 30 minutes. Meanwhile, peel, quarter and core the apples and then cut them into very thin slices straight into a bowl, mixing the two varieties together.

Pre-heat the oven to gas mark 7, 425°F (220°C). Next take a little less than half of the pastry and roll it out very thinly to about 12 inches (30 cm) in diameter to line the base and sides of the pie dish. Trim the edges and leave unused pastry aside for the trimming. Then scatter the semolina over the base of the pastry and after that pile in the apple slices, building up the layers closely and scattering in the sugar and spices as you go. Then press and pack the apples tightly.

Now roll the remaining pastry out, again very thinly, to make the lid, this time 16 inches (40 cm) in diameter. Brush the rim of the base pastry with a little beaten egg and carefully lift the lid over the top. Press the edges together to get a good seal all round, then trim using a knife. Finally gather up the trimmings and re-roll them to cut out into leaf or round shapes if you like. Brush the surface of the pie with beaten egg, make a small hole in the centre the size of a 10p piece (to allow the steam to escape) and arrange the leaves on top.

Now using the back of a small knife 'knock up' the edges then flute them using your thumb and the back of a knife. Now brush the whole lot with beaten egg then place the pie on the baking sheet and bake on a high shelf for 10 minutes. After that reduce the temperature to gas mark 5, 375°F (190°C) and cook for a further 45 minutes or until it has turned a deep golden brown. Then remove the pie and allow it to stand for at least 20 minutes before serving.

Chocolate mayonnaise cake

I know, it sounds totally bonkers to put mayonnaise in a cake. With mayo being made from eggs and oil it makes the cake seriously scrummy. Try it...go on, I dare you...

Ingredients
325g/11 ½ oz mayonnaise
450g/15 ¾ oz plain flour (all-purpose flour)
325g/11 ½ oz sugar
45g/1 ½ oz cocoa powder
2 ¼ teaspoons baking powder
1 ½ teaspoons bicarbonate soda
2 teaspoons vanilla extract
300ml/10 ½ fl oz water

Buttercream frosting/filling:
250g/9 oz butter
400g/14 oz icing sugar (powdered sugar)
1 tablespoon cocoa powder

Method
Preheat the oven to 350F/180C/gas 4.

Grease to 9" cake tins.

Mix together the flour, sugar, cocoa, baking powder, vanilla and bicarbonate of soda. Add in the mayonnaise, stirring to combine. Slowly mix in the water. Mix until smooth.

Pour equally into both pans.

Bake for half an hour.

Whisk the butter, icing sugar and cocoa together until light and fluffy. Fill and top your sponge cake.

Chai cupcakes (vegan)

I love a spiced chai latte, and this brings all those flavours and puts it into cupcake form.

Ingredients
170g/6 oz almond or soya milk
225g/8 oz plain flour (all-purpose flour)
225g/8 oz sugar
1 teaspoon bicarbonate soda
½ teaspoon salt
110g/4 oz vegetable oil
2 tablespoon cider vinegar
2 teaspoons vanilla extract
1 teaspoon cinnamon
½ teaspoon ground cloves
½ teaspoon ground nutmeg
4 cardamom pods, ground

Frosting:
150g/5 ¼ oz margarine (vegan or other)
350g/12 ¼ oz icing sugar (powdered sugar)
1 teaspoon vanilla extract
½ teaspoon ground cinnamon

Method
Preheat the oven to 350F/180C/Gas 4.

Line a cupcake tray with paper cases, you should get 12 from this recipe.

Mix together the flour, sugar, bicarbonate soda, spices and salt. In a separate bowl whisk together the milk, oil, vinegar and vanilla. Pour the wet ingredients into the dry and whisk until combined, be careful not to over mix.

Fill the cake cases about two thirds full. Bake for about 20 minutes. Cool.

To make the frosting whisk the margarine, sugar, cinnamon and vanilla together until light and fluffy. Ice your cupcakes.

Spring cookies

These super yummy cookies have all the promise of spring.

Ingredients
125g/4 ½ oz butter, softened
75g/2 ½ oz caster sugar plus extra for sprinkling
1 egg, separated
200g/7 oz plain flour (all-purpose flour)
Pinch salt
½ teaspoon baking powder
1 teaspoon mixed spice
60g/2 oz sultanas or raisins
1 teaspoon finely chopped mixed peel
1-2 tablespoons milk

Method
Preheat your oven to 400F/200C/Gas 6.

Grease two baking sheets.

Beat the butter until creamy then gradually add the sugar, continuing to beat until the mixture is light and fluffy. Add the egg yolk and whisk again. Add in the flour salt, baking powder and spice, stir until combined. Pop in the sultanas and peel, bring the dough together. If the dough is a little too dry add a tablespoon of milk.

Turn out onto a lightly floured surface and roll out until it is about 5mm/¼ inch thick. Cut into rounds with a cookie cutter. Place them onto the baking sheet spaced apart.

Bake for 10 minutes, until firm and pale golden.

Take the cookies out of the oven and brush each one with egg white and sprinkle the top with a little caster sugar. Return the cookies to the oven and bake for a further 3 minutes until the tops are golden and crunchy.

Options

Replace the mixed spice with cinnamon.
Substitute the mixed peel for fennel seeds.

Anise cookies

This recipe has a simple list of ingredients, but the spice just adds a lovely taste.

Ingredients
200g/7 oz butter
120g/4 ¼ oz sugar
1 egg
465g/16.4 oz plain (all purpose) flour
1 ½ teaspoons crushed anise seed (or fennel seed)
1 ½ teaspoons baking powder
236ml/8.3 ml milk
½ teaspoon salt
Cinnamon and sugar to dust

Method
Preheat the oven to 350F/180C/Gas 4.

Cream the butter, sugar and egg until light and fluffy.

In a separate bowl mix the remaining ingredients then add the creamed butter/sugar mixture.

Gradually add the milk a little at a time until the mixture becomes a soft but stiff dough.

Roll out the dough on a lightly floured board and cut out cookie shapes. Dip the cookies into a mixture of equal amounts of cinnamon and sugar.

Place the cookies on a greased baking sheet and bake for 12-15 minutes or until golden.

Greek bougatsa (custard pie with filo and cinnamon)

This is an amazing custard tart. I have used shop bought filo pastry because, seriously, it is not something you want to be making at home.

Ingredients
450g/15 ¾ oz filo pastry sheets
200g/7 oz melted butter
1kg/35 oz milk
200g/7 oz sugar
120g/4 ¼ oz plain flour (all-purpose flour)
4 eggs
1 teaspoon vanilla extract
Ground cinnamon and icing sugar to top

Method
Start by making the filling, pop the sugar, eggs and flour into a large bowl and whisk together. In a saucepan put the milk and vanilla extract and bring to the boil. Just before the milk boils stir a few spoonfuls of the hot milk into the flour mixture and stir. Turn down the heat and add the flour mixture to the saucepan of milk. Whisk quickly over the heat until the mixture has thickened. This will take a couple of minutes. Remove from the heat and set aside but stir occasionally to stop a skin from forming.

Brush the bottom and sides of a large baking dish/pan with melted butter. Use 5 or 6 sheets of filo to cover the bottom of the dish, brushing each layer with melted butter. Tip the custard mixture over the bottom layers of filo. Top with 4 or 5 more sheets of filo, brushing with butter between each layer. Fold the excess filo edges over the top of the pie. If you have any spare sheets, scrunch some up and use to decorate the top of the pie, brush with plenty of melted butter. Bake the bougatsa in a preheated oven 325F/170C/Gas 3 for 45 minutes until the pastry is crisp and golden.

Allow to cool then sprinkle icing sugar and ground cinnamon on the top before serving.

Red velvet hot chocolate

How cool is this? Hot chocolate but a red velvet version, classy.

Ingredients
500ml/1-pint milk
4 squares dark chocolate
½ teaspoon red food colouring

Topping:
2 tablespoons sugar
240g/ 8.4 fl oz whipping/double cream (heavy)
3 tablespoons cream cheese

Method
Whip together the cream and sugar until stiff then add in the cream cheese and whisk until blended.

Warm the milk in a saucepan with the squares of chocolate until just before boiling, stirring until the chocolate has dissolved, just before you take it off the heat add in the red food colouring.

Pour into a mug and top with the cream cheese mixture.

April

Roasted leek, carrot and cauliflower soup
Cottage pie with cauliflower and potato mash
Cauliflower burger
Vegetable pelau
Sausage gravy and biscuits
Salt and pepper soda bread
Cheese, bacon and rosemary loaf
Spiced fruit buns
Double chocolate American stack pancakes
Lemon drizzle tray bake
Basic vegan chocolate muffins
Anzac cookies
Cardamom cookies
Boozy hot chocolate

April is a lovely month particularly for those that like to garden (that includes me). The end of March/beginning of April will find me outside in my small back garden tidying up and preparing for the new season. If we are lucky the weather starts to improve, and we even get some pretty warm days. Spring has most definitely sprung, and Mother Nature is showing signs all around us. A sneak peek into the bounty of wonderful produce that is in store for us.

This is a basic list of produce that is usually in season during the month of April. It will obviously vary depending on where you are in the world and what the weather has been like. Be guided by what you find in your local greengrocers or farmers market. If you shop in the supermarket, check for labels that say it is 'new season'.

Cabbage (green), carrots, cauliflower, chives, greens, leeks, lettuce, mushrooms, onions, potatoes, purple sprouting, radish, spinach.

Forced rhubarb, outdoor rhubarb (UK & USA).

Roasted leek, carrot and cauliflower soup

Roasting the veggies before you pop them in adds another dimension of flavour to this soup.

Ingredients
3 large carrots, peeled and cut into chunks
2 leeks, cleaned, trimmed and cut into chunks
½ a cauliflower, cut into florets
1 large onion
3 cloves garlic, unpeeled
3 tablespoons olive or vegetable oil
1 litre/35 fl oz vegetable stock
Large handful fresh parsley or 1 teaspoon dried parsley
3 tablespoons balsamic vinegar
Salt and pepper

Method
Preheat the oven to 230C/450F/Gas 8.

Prepare the vegetables, peel and quarter the onion. Pop all the vegetables into a large roasting tin and drizzle over the oil. Give them a stir so that they are all coated well. Drop the garlic cloves into a corner of the tin. Roast in the oven for half an hour to forty minutes, until they start to brown.

Pour the stock into a large pan. Squeeze the roasted garlic pulp from the bulbs into the stock. Add salt and pepper and the parsley. Add in the vegetables and simmer for about an hour. Remove from the heat and stir in the balsamic vinegar.

Blitz the soup in a food processor or blender. Reheat and serve.

Options
Leave out the cauliflower and add in an extra carrot and leek.
Replace the cauliflower with squash or broccoli.

Cottage pie with cauliflower and potato mash

I love cottage pie; it is one of my favourite comfort foods. Cottage pie is the name for this dish when you use beef mince, if you use lamb mince then the name changes to Shepherd's pie. This version adds cauliflower into the potato mash on the top.

Ingredients
450g/15 ¾ oz potatoes
450g/15 ¾ oz cauliflower
2 medium onions, chopped
2 large carrots, chopped
750g/1 ½ lbs beef mince
1 tablespoon plain/all-purpose flour
1 tablespoon tomato puree
A big dollop of butter
Splash of milk
A bay leaf
Worcestershire sauce
1 teaspoon dried thyme or a few sprigs of fresh
250ml /9 fl oz beef stock (a stock cube dissolved in water is fine)
Salt & pepper

Method
Cut the potatoes into chunks (I don't peel them, but you can if you prefer) and break the cauliflower into florets. These can go in a pan of water together, cook until tender (about fifteen minutes). When they are cooked drain them and pop the butter in. Mash together. If it is a bit dry add a splash of milk or more butter. Season with salt and pepper.

In a large pan, brown the beef mince, pop in the diced onions and carrots and simmer for ten minutes. Add in the tomato puree and the flour. Drop in the bay leaf and the thyme. Season with salt and pepper. Splash in a dash or two of Worcestershire sauce. Pour in the stock.

Bring up to heat and simmer gently for about half an hour.

Pre-heat the oven to 190C/375F/Gas 5.

Pop the beef mixture into a casserole dish and top with spoonfuls of the mash. Bake in the oven for twenty-five minutes, until it is a nice golden brown on top.

Options

Use lamb instead of beef mince to make it a Shepherd's pie.

Add in a teaspoon of chilli powder to spice it up.

Give it a twist with a teaspoon of curry powder.

Make it vegetarian by replacing the beef with soya mince, red lentils or diced butternut squash. Replace the Worcestershire sauce with a teaspoon of yeast extract.

Replace the cauliflower with parsnips.

Replace the potatoes with sweet potato.

Cauliflower burger

I love a good veggie burger, but only if it is actually made with vegetables. I have yet to eat a good burger made from soya mince, it just doesn't do it for me. This however is scrummy, particularly if you serve it with all the usual burger fixings; avocado slices, halloumi cheese and caramelised onions of course!

Ingredients
1 medium cauliflower head, cut into florets
2 tablespoon oil (vegetable, olive or coconut)
Salt and pepper
½ teaspoon ground cumin
1 tin pinto or cannelloni beans
1 spring onion (scallion), finely chopped
2 teaspoons coriander (cilantro)
1 teaspoon chilli powder
60g/2 oz cornmeal

Method
Place the cauliflower florets in a food processor and pulse until they look like rice/large breadcrumbs.

Heat 1 tablespoon of the oil in a large pan and add the cauliflower, salt and pepper and cumin. Stir regularly, sauté for about five minutes. Pop the mixture into a bowl and set aside.

Using the same pan, heat the remaining oil and add the beans, onions and coriander. Cook for about five minutes. Pop this all into the food processor and pulse to a smooth texture.

Add the bean mixture to the cauliflower and combine. Let this sit for about ten minutes.

Preheat the oven to 190C/375F/Gas 5.

Line a roasting tin with baking parchment.

Now take scoops of the bean/cauliflower mixture and form them into burgers, you should get six to eight from this mixture.

Place them on the baking sheet and cook in the oven for about 45 minutes.

Options

Use kidney beans or a tin of refried beans instead of pinto.
Add a chopped chilli to ramp up the heat.

Vegetable pelau

This is so simple but very delicious - you can vary the vegetables used depending on what you have or what needs using up.

Ingredients
1 tablespoon olive or vegetable oil
1 tablespoon brown sugar
340g/12 oz brown rice
1 large onion, sliced
2 crushed garlic cloves
2 carrots, diced
2 handfuls of mange tout, chopped
2 bell peppers, sliced
Handful mushrooms, sliced
1 tin chopped tomatoes
1 teaspoon dried thyme
400ml/14 fl oz coconut milk
150ml/5 fl oz vegetable stock
Salt & pepper

Method
Heal the oil in a large pan over a low heat and add the brown sugar, let it melt and turn dark brown, swirl the pan around to avoid it sticking then stir the rice in.

Add all the vegetables, thyme and salt and pepper.

Pour in the coconut milk and stock and bring it all to the boil. Reduce the heat, cover and simmer for about half an hour until the rice is tender.

Option
A dash of hot pepper/chilli sauce can be added with the stock if you like things a bit spicy.

Sausage gravy and biscuits

I have never seen these on a UK menu but was intrigued...we really don't know what we are missing! The biscuits are actually what we would call savoury scones in the UK and the gravy is a sausage flavour béchamel - delicious.

Ingredients

Biscuits:
400g/14 oz plain (all purpose) flour
2 tablespoons baking powder
½ teaspoon salt
170g/6 oz cold butter, diced
100-150g/3 ½ - 5 ¼ oz buttermilk or natural yogurt

Sausage gravy:
450g/15 ¾ oz sausage meat
50g/1 ¾ oz plain (all purpose) flour
900ml/30.4 fl oz milk
½ teaspoon paprika
2 teaspoons ground black pepper

Method
For the biscuits:
Preheat oven to 400F/200C/Gas 6 degrees.
Add flour, baking powder and salt to the bowl of a food processor (or a large bowl.) Add butter pieces and pulse until butter is completely cut into the flour mixture (or use a pastry cutter if using a bowl.) While pulsing (or stirring) drizzle in the buttermilk (or yogurt) until dough just comes together and is no longer crumbly.
Drop spoonfuls on two baking sheets and then bake for 15-17 minutes, or until golden brown.

For the sausage gravy:

Tear small pieces of sausage meat and drop them in a single layer into a large frying pan, fry over a medium high heat until the meat is all browned. Reduce the heat to medium low and sprinkle over half the flour, stir until it soaks into the sausage meat then add the remainder, cook for another minute or two then slowly pour in the milk stirring continually.

Cook the gravy, stirring frequently, until it thickens. (This may take a good 10-12 minutes.) Sprinkle in the paprika and pepper and continue cooking until very thick. If it gets too thick too soon, just splash in another drop of milk.

Spoon sausage gravy over warm biscuits and serve immediately.

Salt and pepper soda bread

Soda bread doesn't use yeast, so it is really quick and easy to make.

Ingredients
225g/8 oz wholemeal or buckwheat flour
2 teaspoons baking powder
½ teaspoon salt
1 teaspoon brown sugar
25g/0.8 oz butter
150ml/5 fl oz milk (any kind)
Teaspoon freshly ground black pepper
A few porridge oats

Method
Preheat the oven to 400F/200C/Gas 6. Grease a baking tray.
Mix together the flour, baking powder, salt, pepper and sugar.
    Rub in the butter. Add in the milk and mix together to form a
    soft dough. Shape into a round and pop onto the baking tray.
Brush the top with milk and sprinkle over a few oats. Bake for
    about 25 minutes until well risen and nicely browned.

Cheese, bacon and rosemary loaf

Using up some left-over gammon instead of the bacon I made this cheesy loaf, although not really bread it is more of a savoury cake but works very well.

Ingredients
Butter, for greasing
4 rashers streaky bacon or pancetta
275g/9 ¾ oz plain flour (all purpose)
1 level tablespoon baking powder
1 teaspoon salt
Pinch of English mustard powder
50g/1 ¾ oz mature cheese, cheddar works well, cut into 1cm cubes
1 large egg
225ml/8 fl oz milk
2 teaspoons finely chopped rosemary

Method
Preheat the oven to 200C/400F/gas 6. Grease the base and sides of a 500g/1 lb loaf tin and line the base with baking parchment.

Snip the bacon into strips and dry fry in a pan until crisp, then cool.

Put the flour, baking powder, salt and mustard powder into a bowl and stir. Add the cheese, bacon, egg, milk and rosemary. Stir well with a wooden spoon until it has a soft dropping consistency - add extra milk, if needed.

Spread in the tin and bake for 25 minutes, until risen, golden brown and just firm to the touch. Serve warm or cold, with butter and cheese, if you like.

Options
If you want to keep it vegetarian, you could leave out the bacon.

Spiced fruit buns

OK so these are really hot cross buns...without the crosses but they taste so yummy...a hot cross bun is not just for Easter, actually buns with crosses on can be found in a lot of cultures.

Ingredients
450g/15 ¾ oz strong white bread flour

50g/1 ¾ oz caster sugar

1 teaspoon salt

2 teaspoons ground mixed spice

½ teaspoon freshly grated nutmeg

7g/2 teaspoons easy blend dried yeast

50g/1 ¾ oz butter, diced

125g/4 ½ oz mixed fruit & peel

200ml/7 fl oz lukewarm milk

2 medium eggs, lightly beaten

2 tablespoons sugar, 4 tablespoon water to glaze

Method

Put the flour, sugar, salt, spices and yeast into a large bowl (or into a food mixer) and mix well. Add the diced butter and rub in until the mixture resembles fine breadcrumbs (I am lazy and do this in the food mixer with the paddle fitted). Stir in the dried fruit.

Pour in the lukewarm milk and the beaten eggs. Bring the mixture together to form a soft dough. Then knead either by hand on a floured surface for ten minutes or in your food mixer with the dough hook for four minutes (on the lowest speed). The dough should be smooth and very elastic.

Place in a bowl and cover with a tea cloth or lid and leave until doubled in size (approx. 1 hour).

Knock back the dough and divide into 12 pieces shaping them into balls.

Set them apart on a greased baking tray and cover, leave to rise again to double in size (about 45 minutes, or you can pop them in the fridge overnight).

Pre-heat the oven to 200C/400F/Gas 6.

Bake in the oven for fifteen minutes, until golden brown.

Dissolve the 2 tablespoons of sugar in 4 tablespoons hot water and use this to brush over the buns as soon as they come out of the oven.

Double chocolate American stack pancakes

Easy to make and fabulous, whether you have them warm with Greek yogurt...OK maybe ice cream...or cold, spread with some butter.

Ingredients
360g/12 ½ oz plain (all purpose) flour
2 ½ teaspoons baking powder
1 tablespoon cocoa powder (sifted)
1 tablespoon chocolate chips (or block chocolate chopped)
1 teaspoon salt
3 large eggs
750ml/26 ½ fl oz milk
6 tablespoons butter
Butter to fry
1 tablespoon honey

Method
Mix the flour, salt and baking powder in a bowl and add the chocolate chips.
In another bowl beat the eggs into the milk.
Melt the 6 tablespoons of butter in a saucepan with the honey, gently until all melted together.
Stir the liquid butter/honey into the milk and eggs.
Add the liquid to the flour mixture and whisk together until the batter is just smooth.
Leave the batter for half an hour.
Melt a teaspoon of butter in a frying pan and ladle on ¼ cup of batter for each pancake. (This mixture makes loads so you will need to do them in batches). Cook for about 30 seconds until small bubbles form on the top of the pancake then turn it over and cook for 30 seconds on the other side.
This mixture makes about 24 pancakes.

Lemon drizzle tray bake

This is a classic cake but works really well as a tray bake. Useful to feed lots of people at a party, event or ritual.

Ingredients
225g/8 oz butter, softened
225g/8 oz caster sugar
275g/9 ¾ oz self-raising flour
2 teaspoons baking powder
4 eggs
4 tablespoons milk
Finely grated rind of 2 lemons

Topping:
175g/6 oz granulated sugar
Juice of 2 lemons

Method
Cut a rectangle of non-stick baking parchment to fit the base and sides of a tray bake tin or roasting tin, 30 x 23 x 4 cm (12 x 9 x 1 ½ inches). Grease the tin and then line with the paper, pushing it neatly into the corners of the tin. Pre-heat the oven to 170C/325F/Gas 3.

Measure all the ingredients for the tray bake into a large bowl and beat well for about 2 minutes until well blended. Turn the mixture into the prepared tin. Level the top gently with the back of the spatula.

Bake in the middle of the pre-heated oven for about 35-40 minutes or until the tray bake springs back when pressed lightly with a finger in the centre and is beginning to shrink away from the sides of the tin.

Allow the tray bake to cool in the tin for a few minutes then lift the tray bake out of the tin still in the lining paper. Carefully remove the paper and put the tray bake onto a wire rack placed over a tray (to catch drips of the topping).

To make the crunchy topping, mix the lemon juice and granulated sugar in a small bowl to give a runny consistency. Spoon this mixture evenly over the tray bake whilst it is still just warm. Cut into about squares when cold.

Options

Try using orange or lime instead of lemon.

Basic vegan chocolate muffins

Add different toppings or fillings such as grated citrus zest or vegan chocolate chips to this basic recipe, but it is delicious just as it is.

Ingredients
225ml/8 fl oz soya or almond milk (if you use dark chocolate almond milk it tastes especially yummy)
1 teaspoon apple cider vinegar
170g/6 oz sugar
70 fl oz/2 ½ fl oz vegetable oil
1 ½ teaspoons vanilla extract
225g/ 8 oz plain (all purpose) flour
70 fl oz/2 ½ oz cocoa powder
¾ teaspoon baking soda
½ teaspoon baking powder
½ teaspoon salt

Method
Preheat the oven to 350F/180C/Gas 4.

Line a 12-hole muffin tin with paper liners.

Whisk together the milk and vinegar and leave to sit for a few minutes so that it slightly curdles. Add in the sugar, oil and vanilla to the milk and beat together until if foams. In a separate bowl mix together the flour, cocoa, baking soda, baking powder and salt. Gradually beat the flour mixture into the wet ingredients until it is well mixed. Spoon into the cake cases. Bake for 15 to 20 minutes.

Anzac cookies

These oat and coconut biscuits apparently hail from Australia and New Zealand and were named in honour of those that fought in World War I. I have taken these to several workshops and I always get asked for the recipe.

Ingredients
150g/5 ¼ oz plain (all purpose) flour
125g/4 ½ oz porridge oats
75g/2 ½ oz desiccated coconut
50g/1 ¾ oz soft light brown sugar
25g/0.8 oz sugar
Pinch salt
125g/4 ½ oz butter
100g/3 ½ oz golden syrup
½ teaspoon bicarbonate of soda
2 tablespoons boiling water

Method
Preheat the oven to 350F/180C/Gas 4 and line two baking sheets with baking parchment.

Mix together the flour, oats, coconut, both sugars and salt.

Melt the butter and golden syrup together in a saucepan over a low heat, remove from the heat and add in the bicarbonate of soda and boiling water, mix quickly to combine.

Pour the melted butter mixture into the dry ingredients and mix until combined. Using your hands roll level tablespoons of the mixture into walnut size balls and arrange on the baking sheets leaving space between each one as they will spread during cooking.

Using the back of a spoon slightly flatten each biscuit and bake in the oven for 12 minutes, until almost firm. The biscuits will crisp up and firm more as they cool.

Cardamom cookies

Called Nankhatai these are a kind of Indian shortbread and recipes vary in that you can add nutmeg or saffron instead of vanilla or use almonds instead of pistachios (or leave the nuts off completely).

Ingredients
125g/4 ½ oz butter, softened
100g/3 ½ oz icing (confectioners) sugar
12 cardamom pods
¼ teaspoon vanilla extract
185g/6 ½ oz plain (all purpose) flour
¼ teaspoon baking powder
40g/1 ½ oz gram flour (chickpea flour)
1 ½ - 2 tablespoons natural yoghurt
20g/ ¾ oz pistachios, chopped

Method
Pre-heat the oven to 170C/325F/Gas 3.

Pop the softened butter into a mixing bowl and beat until creamy. Sift in the icing sugar and beat until the mixture is very light and fluffy.

Remove the seeds from the cardamom pods and finely crush them. Add them to the bowl with the vanilla extract and mix well. Add in the flour, baking powder and gram flour and bring together to form a dough. Mix in 1 ½ tablespoons of the yoghurt to bring it all together, if the mixture is too crumbly add in a dash more yoghurt.

Take a tablespoon of the dough, roll into a ball and place on a baking sheet lined with baking parchment. Repeat until you have used all the dough (you should get approx. 15/16 cookies). Gently flatten the balls so they are about 5cm across. Sprinkle the tops with the pistachios.

Bake in the oven for 20 minutes until firm when pressed gently but still pale in colour. You might need to rotate the baking sheet part way through cooking, so the edges don't catch.

Leave to cool for a couple of minutes then transfer to a wire rack to cool.

Boozy hot chocolate

Take a basic hot chocolate and give it a boozy twist...

Ingredients
284ml/half a pint of milk
Two squares of either dark, milk or plain chocolate
A teaspoon or two of sugar

Method
Warm all the ingredients together in a saucepan. Then add in a
dash of your favourite alcohol, the following work well:

Kahlua
Rum
Tequila
Whisky

And of course, top with whipped cream....

May

Cauliflower soup
Chicken and mustard curry
Potato salad
Crunchy breaded chicken
Bloomer
Spelt loaf
Banana tarte tatin
Floating islands
Lemon and blueberry cake
Courgette (zucchini) and carrot cupcakes
Oat shortbread
Apricot cookies
French custard tart
Mint hot chocolate

May is a month in between, the end of spring and the hint of summer. It also heralds the pagan fire festival of Beltane. The 1st May is all about love, fertility and magic with maidens dancing around the May pole with flowers in their hair, it is a celebration of life.

Food to celebrate this sabbat usually comes from the dairy (milk, butter, cheese etc) especially sweet kinds like custard and ice cream along with honey, oats, fresh fruit, salads, spring vegetables and herbs (such as coriander and marjoram), and fruit punch. I like to add chocolate into this one too, well I like to add it into most festivals...

This is a basic list of produce that is usually in season during the month of May. It will obviously vary depending on where you are in the world and what the weather has been like. Be guided by what you find in your local greengrocers or farmers market. If you shop in the supermarket, check for labels that say it is 'new season'.

Cabbage (green), carrots, cauliflower, chives, greens, lettuce, onions, peas, potatoes, radish, spinach.

Apricots, outdoor rhubarb (UK).

Apricots, cherries, mangoes, pineapples, rhubarb, strawberries (USA).

Cauliflower soup

This is so simple but incredibly delicious. Cauliflower always makes such a good texture for a soup.

Ingredients
1 large onion, chopped
2 medium cauliflowers
4 rashers bacon OR0 2 large handfuls of mushrooms
2 cloves garlic, crushed
2 bay leaves
Oil for frying
1 teaspoon paprika
1 litre/35 fl oz vegetable stock

Method
Chop the bacon and fry until well cooked. If you are not using bacon, slice the mushrooms and fry them in oil until nicely cooked. Add the chopped onion and cook for two to three minutes. Add the crushed garlic and cook for a further couple of minutes. Break the cauliflower into florets and add to the onion mixture. Pour in the stock and add the bay leaves and paprika. Simmer for about half an hour, until the cauliflower is tender.

Remove from the heat, discard the bay leaves and blitz in a food processor or blender. Season with salt and pepper. Reheat and serve.

Options
If you want to keep it vegetarian/vegan, then replace the bacon with mushrooms.
Sprinkle a handful of toasted hazelnuts on top to finish.
Give it a kick of heat by adding in a chopped chilli when you cook the onion.

Chicken and mustard curry

The secret to a good curry is the blend of spices that you use, some recipes have a huge list, this one isn't so bad. It is however, delicious. Serve with rice or naan bread.

Ingredients
3 tablespoons vegetable oil
A chicken jointed or 4 breasts (whichever you prefer)
A teaspoon cumin seeds
2 teaspoons coriander seeds
2 teaspoons mustard seeds
Piece of root ginger (about 2"), grated
3 onions, sliced
2 cloves garlic, crushed
1 teaspoon ground turmeric
1 teaspoon chilli flakes or a large fresh chilli, finely chopped
A tin (425g) chopped tomatoes
1 tin (400g) coconut milk
3 bell peppers, sliced
Salt

Method
Lightly brown the chicken in the oil in a large pan. Lift the chicken out and set aside. Grind the cumin, mustard and coriander seeds lightly. Use a pestle and mortar or the end of a rolling pin in bowl. Re-heat the pan you used for the chicken and add the ground spices. Add the chilli flakes or fresh chilli and the ginger. Pop in the sliced onions and peppers. Simmer for five minutes. Add in the crushed garlic along with the turmeric, tomatoes and a little salt. Simmer for a further five minutes. Return the chicken to the pan and add the coconut milk. Cover partly with a lid and simmer for about half an hour, until the chicken is cooked.

Options

Throw in a handful of green beans or replace the bell pepper with green beans.

To make it hotter, double the amount of chilli.

To make this vegetarian/vegan replace the chicken with tofu or cubed butternut squash.

Potato salad

This is a good basic potato salad recipe that you can switch up with your own variations. If you use soya yogurt this works for vegans.

Ingredients
500g/1 lb new potatoes
60g/2 oz natural yogurt
2 tablespoons lemon juice
2 tablespoons mustard
4 spring onions
Tablespoon dill
160g/5 ½ oz spinach leaves
Olive oil

Method
Cut the potatoes in half, keeping the skin on. Boil in salted water until just tender (10-15 mins). Drain.

Wash the spinach and pat dry, pop into a bowl and add a drizzle of olive oil and season with salt and pepper. Add in the potatoes.

Chop the dill and spring onions and add to the potatoes.

Mix together the yoghurt and mustard, add in the lemon juice and season with salt and pepper. Mix and then pour over the potatoes. Stir everything gently together.

Options
Leave out the spinach.
Use mayonnaise instead of yogurt.
Replace the spring onions with sliced red onion.
Add in sliced boiled eggs.
Replace the dill with chopped parsley or chives.
Use sweet potatoes or butternut squash instead of potato.

Leave out the yogurt and just use olive oil instead.
Add in a handful of peas when you are cooking the potatoes.
Stir in cooked mackerel or tuna fish at the end.
Add in green beans when you are cooking the potatoes.
Pop in a handful of sliced radishes.

Crunchy breaded chicken

Basically, large and slightly up market chicken nuggets.

Ingredients
2 large chicken breasts, skin removed
2 medium eggs
Salt & pepper
150g/5 ¼ oz breadcrumbs
1 tablespoon dried herbs (oregano, parsley, thyme)
Olive oil

Method
Slice each chicken breast horizontally across the middle to make
   four fillets. Place each piece one at a time between two sheets
   of baking parchment and using the end of a rolling pin pound
   each fillet until it is about 0.5cm thick.
In a shallow dish beat the eggs and season with salt and pepper.
Pop the breadcrumbs in another dish and add the herbs.
Take each piece of chicken and dip it first in the egg then in the
   herby breadcrumbs to coat.
Put some oil in a large frying pan over a medium heat. Cook the
   chicken for 2-5 minutes on each side until cooked through.

Bloomer

This is a lovely recipe that makes a wonderful loaf...warning...it will be eaten within minutes!

Ingredients
500g/1 lb strong white flour, plus extra for kneading
10g/¼oz salt
7g sachet/2 teaspoons of instant yeast
320ml/11½oz cold water
40ml/1½fl oz olive oil, plus extra for kneading
Extra oil and flour, for kneading

Method
Place the dry ingredients in a bowl, taking care not to have the salt and yeast touching. Add the oil and 240ml/9fl oz of water.

Using your hands, mix the ingredients together. Gradually add the remaining water (you may not need it all), until all the flour leaves the side of the bowl and you have a soft, rough dough.

Pour a little oil onto a clean work surface. Sit the dough on the oil and begin to knead. Do this for 5-10 minutes, or until the dough becomes smooth and silky. Once the correct consistency is achieved, place the dough into a clean, oiled bowl. Cover with cling film and leave in a warm place until tripled in size.

Once risen, place the dough onto a floured surface. Knock the dough back by folding it in on itself repeatedly. Do this until all the air is knocked out and the dough is smooth.

To shape into the bloomer, flatten the dough into a rectangle. With the long side facing you fold each end into the middle then roll like a Swiss roll so that you have a smooth top with a seam along the base. Very gently roll with the heel of your hands.

Place on a tray lined with parchment paper, cover and leave to prove for 1-2 hours at room temperature, or until doubled in size.

Lightly spray with water and dust with a little flour. Make four diagonal slashes using a sharp knife across the top.

Preheat the oven to 220/425F/Gas 7 and place a baking tray filled with water on the bottom shelf of the oven - this will create steam when the loaf is baking. Place the loaf on the middle shelf and bake for 25 minutes. After this time lower the heat to 200C/400F/Gas 6 and bake for a further 10 minutes. Remove from the oven and leave to cool on a wire rack.

Spelt loaf

Spelt flour is one of the ancient grains. This loaf is delicious...

Ingredients
1 heaped teaspoon dried yeast
30 ml/10.6 fl oz tepid water
250g/9 oz wholemeal spelt flour
250g/9 oz strong white bread flour, plus extra for dusting
1 heaped teaspoon salt
Sea salt for sprinkling

Method
Mix the yeast and tepid water until the yeast has dissolved. Combine the flours in a bowl, add the dissolved yeast and the salt, and bring together into a dough. Tip it out on to the work surface and knead vigorously for 15 minutes to make a soft, stretchy dough.

Transfer to a bowl and cover it. Allow to prove until doubled in size (no more than 1 hour), in a warm place.

Grease a large (2lb) loaf tin. Once the dough is proved, shape it gently to fit the tin. Place it in the tin, cover and leave to prove for a further hour or until doubled in size.

Pre heat your oven to 450F/230C/Gas 8.

Sprinkle the loaf with spelt flour and sea salt. Spray the oven with water spray and close the door to create a crust. Bake for 30 minutes.

Banana tarte tatin

Bananas, caramel and pastry - what's not to love? Delicious!

Ingredients

For the rough puff pastry: (or you could use shop bought):
225g/8 oz plain (all purpose) flour, plus extra for dusting
pinch salt
190g/6 ½ oz unsalted butter, cold, cut into 2cm/¾in cubes
½ tbsp lemon juice

For the caramel:
100g/3 ½ oz granulated white sugar
60g/2 oz salted butter

For the topping:
3 firm bananas

Method

For the rough puff pastry, sift the flour and salt into a large bowl
and add the butter. Move the butter around until coated in
the flour.

Mix 125ml/4.3 fl oz of water and the lemon juice together in a jug
and pour into the flour and butter. Using a butter knife, mix
in the liquid and chop the butter slightly as you go, turning
the bowl round, until the ingredients have combined into a
dough.

On a floured work surface, tip the dough out and quickly shape
it into a block. Roll out the dough into a rectangle roughly
35cmx20cm/14inx8in in size. With the short side of the pastry
rectangle in front of you, fold the bottom third of the pastry
to the middle, then fold the top half down to cover it. Roll
the pastry out into a rectangle again and repeat the folding

process. Turn the pastry a quarter turn and roll out and fold again. Repeat this 4-5 times.

After the last folding, wrap the pastry in cling film and leave to chill in the fridge for a few hours, or preferably overnight. When the pastry has chilled, preheat the oven to 180C/350F/ Gas 4.

Caramel can be a tricky beastie to make so I have put two versions here, the first is more difficult the second is a lot easier:

Caramel option 1:

To make the caramel, heat the sugar with a tablespoon of water in an ovenproof frying pan over a low heat and slowly bring to the boil. Keep boiling until the syrup turns a light golden colour - this will take between 5-7 minutes. Add the butter in and swirl the pan (don't stir) until it has all melted. Remove from the heat and leave to cool for a few minutes.

Caramel option 2:

Using 90g/3oz of butter and 90g/3oz demerara sugar - put them both in a pan and heat gently until the sugar dissolves then increase the heat and cook for 4-5 minutes until the mixture turns dark brown and is thick but pourable.

Slice the bananas into rounds and arrange in a pattern on the caramel.

Roll out the pastry and cut out a circle slightly bigger than your pan. Place the pastry on top of the bananas and tuck it in around the edges. Pierce the top of the pastry with a fork and place in the pre heated oven for 40-45 minutes, or until the pastry is golden and puffed up. Immediately turn the tart out onto a plate (take care as the caramel will still be very hot and may splash) and serve.

Floating islands (Îles flottantes)

I first had these on my honeymoon...in Paris...on a boat...on the river.

Ingredients

For the crème anglaise:
4 eggs - yolks only
80g/2 ¾ oz sugar
1 vanilla pod, seeds scraped out (or 1 teaspoon vanilla extract)
500ml/1-pint milk

For the meringue islands:
2 eggs, whites only (60g/2 oz)
45g/1 ½ oz icing sugar (powdered sugar)
couple of drops of lemon juice
Pinch of salt

For the caramel:
I usually cheat and use a jar of caramel sauce, but if you want to be fancy, use the caramel recipe included with the tarte tatin recipe in this book.

Method
To make the crème anglaise, mix the egg yolks and sugar together in a bowl.

Place the vanilla pod and seeds in a pan with the milk and pepper and bring to a boil.

Remove the pod (you can rinse and dry it and use for vanilla sugar). Then pour a little of the hot milk onto the egg yolk mixture, whisking continuously.

Gradually whisk in the rest of the milk, then pour the mix into a clean pan, set over a gentle heat and whisk constantly. Do not let the custard simmer at any point or it will split.

After five minutes it will begin to thicken slightly and become the consistency of single cream (it will thicken more when it cools down).

Transfer to a bowl and chill in the fridge for at least four hours.

To make the meringue islands, put half the egg whites into a clean glass or metal bowl.

Add the sugar, lemon juice and salt and whisk until snow white.

Add the rest of the egg whites and continue whisking until the meringue forms stiff peaks when the whisk is removed.

Gently drop six spoonfuls of meringue into a large pot of simmering water and simmer for a few minutes or until they are slightly puffed up and just set. Remove with a slotted spoon and place onto a sheet of baking paper until needed.

To assemble, pour a ladleful of crème anglaise into each of six glasses and gently place a meringue in the centre. Drizzle with caramel sauce.

Lemon and blueberry cake

Fresh zingy lemons and luscious blueberries come together to make this a real 'herald the start of summer' cake.

Ingredients
225g/8 oz butter, softened
225g/8 oz sugar
4 large eggs
225g/8 oz self-raising flour
2 level teaspoons baking powder
Zest of two lemons
200g/7 oz lemon curd
350g/12 ¼ oz mascarpone
Punnet of blueberries

Method
Preheat the oven to 350F/180C/Gas 4.

Lightly grease two 8inch sandwich tins and line the base with baking parchment.

Pop the butter, sugar, eggs, flour, lemon zest and baking powder into a bowl and beat for a couple of minutes until blended.

Divide the mixture between the prepared tins and level the surface. Bake for about 25 minutes until well risen and golden. Leave the cakes to cool for a couple of minutes in the tin before turning out onto a wire rack, leave to cool completely.

Make the filling; Whisk the lemon curd and mascarpone together until thick then chill until needed.

Lay one of the cakes on your serving plate and fill with half of the curd and mascarpone mix, you can pipe this or spread it with a knife, sprinkle with a handful of blueberries then put the other half of the cake on top. Spread or pipe the remaining mascarpone mix on top of the cake and decorate with more blueberries.

Options
Substitute raspberries for blueberries.

Courgette (zucchini) and carrot cupcakes (vegan)

A spin on the traditional carrot cake recipe that evolved because I had started making them when I realised I didn't have enough carrots, but I did have a courgette...some of the best recipes are born from necessity!

Ingredients
350g/12 ¼ oz plain flour (all-purpose flour)
250g/9 oz sugar
1 teaspoon baking powder
½ teaspoon bicarbonate soda
1 teaspoon salt
1 teaspoon ground cinnamon
½ teaspoon ground nutmeg
½ teaspoon ground ginger
225ml/8 fl oz orange juice
100ml/3 ½ fl oz vegetable oil
1 tablespoon cider vinegar
1 teaspoon vanilla extract
2 carrots, peeled and grated
1 courgette (zucchini), grated
150g/5 ¼ oz sultanas

Frosting:
150g/5 ¼ oz margarine (vegan or other)
350g/12 ¼ oz icing sugar (powdered sugar)
1 teaspoon vanilla extract

Method
Preheat the oven to 350F/180C/Gas 4.

Line two cupcake trays with paper cases, you should get 14-16 from this recipe.

Mix together the flour, sugar, baking powder, bicarbonate soda, salt and spices. In a separate bowl whisk together the orange juice, oil, vinegar and vanilla. Pour the wet ingredients into the dry and whisk until combined. Be careful not to over mix. Gently fold in the carrots, courgette and sultanas.

Spoon into the cases, about two thirds full and bake for 20 minutes. Cool.

To make the frosting whisk the margarine, sugar and vanilla together until light and fluffy. Ice your cupcakes.

Oat shortbread (vegan option)

Simple, easy but oh, so delicious. Excellent to accompany a cuppa but also on picnics or for rituals.

Ingredients
275g/9 ¾ oz porridge oats
100g/3 ½ oz plain flour (all-purpose flour)
150g/5 ¼ oz caster sugar
½ teaspoon bicarbonate soda
1 level teaspoon salt
225g/8 oz butter, softened (vegan option)

Method
Preheat your oven to 350F/180C/Gas 4.

Give the oats a whizz in the processor until they are fine. Pop all the ingredients into a bowl and mix until it comes together as a dough.

On a lightly floured surface roll out the dough to about 5mm/ ¼" thickness. Cut out with a cookie cutter and place on a baking sheet (no need to grease or line).

Bake for 15-20 minutes until pale golden.

Options
Add 1 teaspoon ground cinnamon.
Add 1 teaspoon fennel or sesame seeds.
Pop in the zest of an orange, lime or a lemon.

Apricot cookies

A very adaptable cookie recipe.

Ingredients
100g/3 ½ oz dried apricots, chopped
225g/8 oz butter at room temperature
125g/4 ½ oz icing sugar (powdered sugar)
2 medium egg yolks
1 teaspoon vanilla extract
300g/10 ½ oz plain (all purpose) flour
Pinch of salt

Method
Cream the butter and icing sugar together until pale and light. Add the egg yolks one at a time mixing well, then add in the vanilla extract.

Pop the salt and flour into the bowl and mix until almost combined. Add in the chopped apricots and mix again until thoroughly combined.

Lightly flour your work surface and hands and then shape the dough into a log shape (you might need to do this in two batches, making two logs). Make the log about 4cm (1 ½ inches) in diameter.

Wrap in clingfilm and pop in the fridge for at least one hour, until firm.

Preheat the oven to 180C/350F/Gas 4 and line two baking sheets with baking parchment.

Cut the log into slices, roughly 5mm (¼ inch) thick and lay them on the baking sheets. Bake in the middle of the oven for about 12 minutes until firm and pale golden brown.

Options

I added in chopped dried apricots, but you could use chopped glace cherries, sultanas, candied peel, lemon/orange zest, chocolate chips or even chopped nuts.

French custard tart

The custard sets firmly on this tart, so it makes a good dessert to take on a picnic.

Ingredients

For the pastry:
225g/8 oz plain flour (all purpose)
100g/3 ½ oz butter, diced
Pinch salt
Cold water

For the custard:
3 eggs
60g/2 oz corn flour (corn starch)
100g/3 ½ oz sugar
500ml/1-pint milk
1 teaspoon vanilla extract or one vanilla pod

Method
Preheat oven to 200C/400F/Gas 6.

Make the pastry by rubbing the butter into the flour until it resembles fine breadcrumbs then add in the salt. Add in 1 tablespoon water and mix, gradually add in 1 more tablespoon of water and mix until you have a firm dough. Wrap in cling film and chill for 20 minutes.

Roll out the pastry, then line a tart mould and leave about half an inch over the edge. Put in the fridge.

Meanwhile pour the milk into a pan, add the vanilla and bring to the boil.

Remove from the heat as soon as the mix is boiling, cover and leave to infuse for 15 minutes.

In a separate bowl beat together the eggs and sugar than add in the corn flour and mix thoroughly.

Pour the vanilla milk onto the beaten eggs while gently whisking to mix well.

Clean the pan, then pour the milk back in through a sieve.

Put the pan over a low heat, stirring continuously with a whisk and cook until the mixture thickens slightly.

As soon as the mix is slightly thickened, put the base of the pan into cold water, and continue stirring to halt cooking, until the mixture cools.

Remove the pastry case from the fridge, trim and neaten the edges with a knife and prick all over the pastry case bottom with a fork.

Pour mixture into the pastry case and immediately put in the oven for about 50 minutes.

The tart is ready when the custard has set, the top will have a light brown skin on. Leave to cool before serving.

Mint hot chocolate

Add a touch of after dinner class to your hot chocolate...

Ingredients
500ml/1-pint milk
1 tablespoon sugar
½ teaspoon vanilla extract
4 squares milk, dark or white chocolate
3 springs of fresh mint
Peppermint candy canes

Method
Place the mint leaves into the milk over a low heat in a saucepan until just before it boils, remove from the heat, cover the pan and allow to sit for five minutes.

Remove the mint leaves then return the pan to the heat, add in the squares of chocolate, the sugar and the vanilla extract, stir until the chocolate has melted.

June

Spinach and broccoli soup
Pasta bake
Vegetable and feta pie
Baked polenta
Floury baps
Gluten free brown loaf
Cheese straws
Queen of puddings
Rosemary loaf cake
Basic vegan vanilla cupcakes
Lemon thyme cookies
Scones
Coconut rock buns
Chocolate cream cake
Orange and cardamom hot chocolate

June is a beautiful month, the beginning of summer proper
and the garden is starting to flourish. This month is all about

the abundance of beauty on our planet and a celebration of everything that she provides for us. Ideal food to share is honey, fresh vegetables, citrus fruit, summer fruits, summer squash, salads, herbs (such as basil, fennel, lavender, lemon verbena and thyme), ale and mead and of course if the weather is good ... anything you can throw on the BBQ.

June brings the summer solstice. The longest day and the shortest night of the year. This is a time to celebrate the completion of the cycle that began at the winter solstice - the sun is at the height of its power and although hopefully the hot days of summer are yet to come, this is the point when the year starts to wane.

This is a basic list of produce that is usually in season during the month of June. It will obviously vary depending on where you are in the world and what the weather has been like. Be guided by what you find in your local greengrocers or farmers market. If you shop in the supermarket, check for labels that say it is 'new season'.

Beetroot, broad beans, broccoli, cabbage (green), carrots, cauliflower, chives, courgette/zucchini, cucumber, garlic, lettuce, onions, peas, potatoes, radish, spinach, tomatoes.

Apricots, blackcurrants, cherries, gooseberries, outdoor rhubarb, strawberries (UK).

Apricots, blueberries, cherries, melon, kiwi, mangoes, peaches, strawberries (USA).

Spinach and broccoli soup

Oh, this is such a glorious vibrant green colour! Actually, it would make a good 'wicked witch' soup for Samhain/Halloween too.

Ingredients
2 tablespoons olive or vegetable oil
1 large onion, chopped
2 garlic cloves, crushed
1.5 litres/3 pints vegetable stock
3 large potatoes, diced
2 heads of broccoli, chopped
3 large handfuls of spinach leaves
Salt and pepper

Method
Heat the oil in a pan and sauté the onion and garlic for about five minutes until it starts to soften. Add the stock, potato and broccoli. Simmer for about fifteen minutes, until the vegetables are tender.

Stir in the spinach and cook for a couple of minutes.

Remove from the heat and blitz in a food processor or with a blender. Season with salt and pepper.

Reheat and serve.

Options
Use half broccoli and half cauliflower for a thicker soup.

Pasta bake

I grew up eating this recipe, it was one that I continued to cook once I left home and now my own family love it too.

Ingredients
6 rashers streaky bacon
225g/8 oz penne pasta (or twists or any shape really)
1 onion, chopped
1 clove garlic, crushed
Tin of tomatoes, drained
340g/12 oz grated Cheddar cheese
30g/1 oz butter
3 tablespoons plain flour (all purpose)
475ml/16 ½ fl oz milk
Packet of plain crisps (potato chips), crushed

Method
Preheat oven to 180C/350F/Gas 4.

Chop the bacon and sauté in a pan until cooked.

Cook the pasta in a large pan of salted water, until al dente.

Sauté the chopped onion and garlic. Take off heat and add chopped cooked bacon and set aside.

To make the sauce, in a saucepan melt the butter over a low heat. Once melted, add the flour and stir constantly for 2 minutes. Gradually add milk and continue stirring until thickened. Stir in 2/3 of the grated Cheddar cheese and stir until melted.

Combine cooked pasta, sautéed onions, garlic, bacon and sauce. Add in the drained tomatoes.

Pour into a baking dish, sprinkle the crushed crisps over the top and sprinkle over remaining Cheddar cheese.

Bake uncovered in the preheated oven until cheese on top is melted and brown, 15 to 20 minutes.

Options

To make this vegetarian replace the bacon with sliced mushrooms.

If you are really short of time you can use a jar of bechamel or white lasagne sauce instead of making your own.

Throw in a couple of sliced bell peppers or green beans to add some veggies.

Vegetable and feta pie (Booby Pie)

I was looking for a nice veggie pie recipe and found a pizza pie one...I took inspiration from it and made my own 'vegetable & feta cheese' pie.

I happened to pick up a round cookie cutter to make decorations on the top with left over pastry bits...prompting my husband to say "it looks like a booby pie"...so I present to you... Booby Pie...

Ingredients

Shortcrust pasty:
225g/8 oz plain flour (all purpose)
100g/3 ½ oz butter, diced
Pinch salt
Cold water
I double this quantity to give me enough pastry for decoration and other baking

Filling:
1 tablespoon olive oil
2 courgettes (zucchini), thinly sliced
1 carrot thinly sliced
1 onion thinly sliced
1 large red pepper thinly sliced
2 cloves garlic, crushed
1 sweet potato thinly sliced
½ teaspoon dried oregano
½ teaspoon dried thyme
Salt & Pepper
100g/3 ½ oz feta cheese

Method

Make the pastry by rubbing the butter into the flour until it resembles fine breadcrumbs then add in the salt. Add in 1 tablespoon water and mix, gradually add in 1 more tablespoon of water and mix until you have a firm dough. Wrap in cling film and chill.

Make the filling by heating the oil in a large pan and gently sauté all the vegetables adding in the seasoning and herbs until just cooked. Set the filling aside to cool, it needs to be cold to put in the pastry, if it is too hot it will give you a soggy bottom!

Half the pastry and roll out one piece to fill a flan or pie tin. There is no need to blind bake the pastry case, but I recommend putting it in the fridge for about 20 minutes to settle.

When the filling is cool spread it out onto the pastry case and crumble the feta cheese on top of the vegetables then roll out the other half of the pastry to make the lid. Cut out pastry shapes if you are feeling creative and pop them on the top. Brush the lid with milk if you want to.

Bake in a pre-heated oven (180C/400F/Gas 6) for about half an hour, until the pastry is golden.

Options

Replace the feta with mozzarella.
Use parsnips instead of courgettes.
Use potato instead of sweet potato.

Baked polenta

To be honest I find polenta to be a weird texture, however this dish changed my mind.

Ingredients
1 litre/1 ¾ pints milk
Salt & pepper
300g/10 ½ oz instant polenta or semolina
2 medium egg yolks
100g/3 ½ oz butter
150g/5 ¼ oz grated parmesan cheese

Method
Preheat the oven to 200C/400F/Gas 6.

In a pan bring the milk almost to the boil over a medium heat, season with salt and pepper. Slowly pour in the polenta whisking for a couple of minutes until you have a smooth, thick mixture. Remove from the heat and add the egg yolks, half the butter and half the parmesan cheese.

Sprinkle a little water over a large baking tray then tip the polenta mix onto the tray. Press the mixture flat with your hands or a spoon to a thickness of about 1.5cm. Leave to cool in the fridge for half an hour.

When cool and set, turn out the polenta onto a flat surface and cut out circles with a biscuit cutter (or a glass). Lay the pieces in an over lapping layer in an oven proof dish. I like to use the left-over polenta (that the circles leave behind) on the bottom layer so as not to waste any.

Dot the polenta with the remaining butter, sprinkle with the rest of the cheese and bake for 15-20 minutes until golden brown.

Floury baps

In true British "Carry On" film humour…I have floury baps!

This is my son's favourite recipe to make and is really easy and fun for children to do. It creates very soft squishy and incredibly yummy bread rolls.

Ingredients
1 teaspoon dried yeast
50ml (1 ¾ fl oz) tepid water
250g/9 oz strong white bread flour
1 teaspoon sugar
1 tablespoon butter
1 teaspoon sea salt
100ml (3 ½ fl oz) tepid milk

Method
Stir the yeast into the tepid water and put to one side.

Then put the flour, sugar, butter and salt into a large bowl and add the tepid milk. Then add in the water and yeast mix.

Knead for about 15 minutes.

Leave to rise covered in a warm place for one hour.

Divide the dough into four, shape into balls and then flatten them slight. Place on a greased proof sheet, dust with flour, cover and leave to rise for a further hour.

Then bake in the oven 200C/400F/Gas 6 for 12 minutes.

Gluten free brown loaf

I have been experimenting with gluten free flour. You can buy the flour already blended and you can get premade flour specifically for bread. It has produced some really good results.

Ingredients
500g/1 lb gluten free bread flour
2 teaspoons quick dried yeast
425ml/15 fl oz milk (any kind)
1 teaspoon salt
1 tablespoon sugar
1 teaspoon cider vinegar
6 tablespoons olive oil
2 egg whites

Method
Put the egg whites, vinegar, sugar, salt, milk and oil into a bowl and whisk. Add in the flour and yeast and mix to a smooth, thick batter.
Oil a 1kg/2lb loaf tin and spoon the dough in, levelling the top.
Cover loosely with cling film and leave to rise until the dough reaches the top of the tin (usually about an hour).
Pre heat your oven to 220C/425F/Gas 7.
Bake for 50-60 minutes.

Cheese straws

A must have at any self-respecting picnic or party.

Ingredients
225g/8 oz plain flour (all purpose)
¼ teaspoon salt
¼ teaspoon cayenne pepper
115g/4 oz cold butter, diced
115g/4 oz parmesan or strong cheddar cheese, grated
1 medium egg, beaten plus ½ a beaten egg to glaze

Method
Lightly oil a large baking sheet (you might need two). Pre heat the oven to 200C/400F/Gas 6.

Pop the flour, salt and cayenne pepper into a bowl and rub the butter into the flour until it resembles fine breadcrumbs (I do this in a food processor). Stir in the cheese and the herbs if you are using them. Mix in the egg and add between 2 to 5 tablespoons of cold water, just enough to get the dough to squish together. Turn out onto a floured surface and knead lightly until smooth.

Roll out the dough to 5mm (¼ inch) thick, you may want to cut the dough in half and do this in two lots. Trim the edges and cut into strips about 20cm (8 inches) long and about 1cm (½ inch) wide. Gently twist each strip and lay onto a baking sheet. Re roll the trimmings and repeat until you have used all the dough.

Brush the straws with beaten egg and if using sprinkle with caraway or sesame seeds.

Bake for 15 minutes or until golden brown then cool on a wire rack. They will keep for a few days in an airtight tin...if you don't eat them all first.

Options

Add a teaspoon of oregano or parsley.

Add a teaspoon of caraway or sesame seeds.

Queen of puddings

Memories from my childhood with this one...My grandmother used to make this dessert when we visited for Sunday lunch.

Ingredients

For the base:
500ml/1 pint full-fat milk
25g/0.8 oz butter, plus extra for greasing the dish
50g/1 ¾ oz caster sugar
3 free-range eggs, yolks only
75g/2 ½ oz fresh white breadcrumbs

For the meringue:
175g/6 oz caster sugar
3 free-range eggs, whites only

For the fruit jam:
Half a jar of raspberry jam

Method

Preheat the oven to 170C/325F/Gas 3 and grease a 1.4 litre/2½ pint shallow ovenproof dish (one that will fit into a roasting tin) with butter.

For the base, very gently warm the milk in a small saucepan. Add the butter and the 50g/1 ¾ oz of sugar, stir until dissolved. Lightly whisk the egg yolks in a bowl. Slowly pour the warm milk into the eggs, while whisking.

Sprinkle the breadcrumbs over the base of the buttered dish and pour over the custard. Leave to stand for about 15 minutes, so the breadcrumbs absorb the liquid.

Carefully transfer the dish to a roasting tin and fill the tin halfway with hot water. Bake the custard in the preheated oven for about 25-30 minutes until the custard has set. Remove from the oven and set aside to cool a little.

Whisk the egg whites using an electric hand whisk on full speed until stiff peaks form when the whisk is removed. Add the remaining 175g/6 oz sugar a teaspoon at a time, still whisking on maximum speed until the mixture is stiff and shiny. Transfer the meringue mixture to a piping bag.

Spread 4-5 tablespoons of the fruit jam over the set custard, then pipe the meringue on top.

Lower the oven temperature to 150C/300F/Gas 2 and return the pudding to the oven (not in the roasting tin with water) for about 25-30 minutes until the meringue is pale golden all over and crisp.

Serve at once with pouring cream.

Options

I am the only lover of jam in our house, so I often replace the jam with golden syrup.

Replace the jam with lemon or orange curd.

Use any fruit compote instead of the jam.

Rosemary loaf cake

Weird I know, herbs in a cake? Trust me, it works. This slices really well and makes an excellent addition to picnics or rituals.

Ingredients
250g/9 oz butter at room temperature, diced
200g/7 oz caster sugar
3 large eggs
210g/7.4 oz self-raising flour
90g/3 oz plain flour (all purpose)
½ teaspoon vanilla extract
Leaves from a 10cm stalk of rosemary, chopped
4 tablespoons of milk
2 tablespoons caster sugar, extra.

Method
Preheat oven to 325F/170C/Gas 3 and grease and line a loaf tin.

In a bowl cream the butter and the sugar, continue creaming until smooth and light.

Beat in the eggs one at a time, folding in a heaped spoonful of flour after each addition, and after this is mixed add the rest of the flour, then the vanilla and rosemary.

Add the milk, mix well then spoon into the tin. Sprinkle over the extra sugar then bake for 50-60 minutes/until a skewer comes out clean.

Leave on a wire rack in the tin until cold. Store in an airtight container.

Basic vegan vanilla cupcakes

This is my standard 'go to' recipe for vegan cupcakes, you can tinker with the flavours by adding zest or spices.

Ingredients
225ml/8 fl oz soya or almond milk
1 teaspoon cider vinegar
160g/5 ½ oz plain flour (all purpose)
2 tablespoons cornflour (corn starch)
¾ teaspoon baking powder
½ teaspoon bicarbonate soda
½ teaspoon salt
110g/4 oz vegan margarine or 75g/2 ½ oz vegetable oil
170g/6 oz sugar
2 ½ teaspoons vanilla extract

Method
Preheat your oven to 350F/180C/Gas 4.

Line a muffin tin with 12 paper cases.

Whisk the soya milk and vinegar together, they should curdle.

If you are using margarine: Pop the flour, cornflour, baking powder, bicarbonate soda and salt into a separate bowl. In a large bowl whisk the margarine and sugar together until light and fluffy, this should take a couple of minutes. Beat in the vanilla. Then add the soy milk mixture alternated with the flour mixture.

If you are using oil: Beat together the soya milk mixture, oil, sugar and vanilla. Add in the dry ingredients and mix until smooth.

Fill the cake cases two thirds full.

Bake for 20 minutes.

Options

Add 1 teaspoon cinnamon or mixed spice.

Add the zest of a lemon, lime or an orange.

Add 1 teaspoon coffee or coconut extract.

Fold in two heaped tablespoons chocolate chips or chopped nuts.

Lemon thyme cookies (vegan option)

Summer in cookie form.

Ingredients
300g/10 ½ oz plain flour (all-purpose flour)
80g/2 ¾ oz icing sugar (powdered sugar)
170g/6 oz margarine (vegan option)
¼ teaspoon salt
2 teaspoons chopped thyme leaves
Zest from 4 lemons

Method
Preheat your oven to 350F/180C/Gas 4.

Grease an 8" square baking tin and line with baking parchment. Leave an overhang so you can use the edges to lift the cookies out.

Mix together the flour, sugar, salt, thyme and lemon zest. Add the margarine and mix until combined, it will be a crumbly mixture. Press the dough into the prepared pan and smooth the top.

Bake for 20 minutes until lightly golden around the edges.

Allow it to cool in the tin.

Once cool, lift the parchment paper to release the mixture from the tin.

Cut into squares.

Options
Replace the thyme with basil or rosemary.
Substitute the lemon for orange or lime.

Scones (vegan option)

Summer is for scones; it is the law (or at least it should be). If you use vegan margarine and plant milk, then they are vegan too - and you get the same excellent baking result. Always serve with cream and jam.

Ingredients
225g/8 oz self-raising flour
1 teaspoon baking powder
50g/1 ¾ oz margarine (vegan or softened butter)
25g/0.8 oz sugar
7 tablespoons milk (any kind)
Milk to glaze

Method
Preheat the oven to 220C/425F/Gas 7. Grease a baking sheet.

This is an easy all in one recipe, mix all the ingredients together to form a dough. I do this in the food mixer with the paddle attachment.

Turn the dough onto a lightly floured surface, knead very gently until the dough comes together. Don't over work it.

Roll out to a thickness of about ¾ inch. Don't roll too thinly otherwise the scones won't rise enough.

Cut into rounds. Knead the trimmings together and roll out again to cut the rest.

Place on the baking sheet and brush the tops with milk.

Bake for 12-15 minutes until golden brown.

You will get about 8 scones from this recipe, depending on the size of cutter you use.

Options
Add in a handful of sultanas.
Add in a handful of chopped chocolate (plain, milk or white).

Mix in a teaspoon of ground cinnamon.
Add in a teaspoon of mixed spice.
Add the zest of one orange, lemon or lime.

Coconut rock buns

Called rock buns because you just spoon dollops of them onto a baking tray and they look like rocks, not because they taste like them...

Ingredients
225g/8 oz plain (all purpose) flour
1 teaspoon baking powder
80g/2 ¾ oz butter, cubed
115g/4 oz brown sugar
½ teaspoon mixed spice
Pinch of salt
100g/3 ½ oz desiccated or shredded coconut
80g/2 ¾ oz sultanas or raisins
1 egg, beaten
4 tablespoons milk
50g/1 ¾ oz maraschino cherries, chopped (optional)

Method
Preheat the oven to 180C/350F/Gas 4 and either butter and flour a baking tray or pop a piece of baking parchment on top.

Pop the flour and baking powder into a mixing bowl add the butter and rub together until they resemble breadcrumbs. Add the sugar, mixed spice, salt, coconut, sultanas or raisins and cherries if you are using. Mix well. Add the beaten egg and 2 tablespoons of the milk to bind the ingredients and make a stiff dough, adding the remaining milk if necessary.

Drop 12 spoonfuls of the mixture on to the prepared tray and bake for 20 minutes until golden.

Chocolate cream cake

We made a cake for a big family gathering so we wanted something that was easy to make (and transport in the car) but also looked pretty...

Ingredients
200g/7 oz butter, softened, plus more for the tins
70g/2 ½ oz dark chocolate
55g/2 oz milk chocolate
1 teaspoon instant coffee
200g/7 oz caster sugar
4 large eggs
200g/7 oz plain flour (all purpose)
50g/1 ¾ oz cocoa powder
1 ½ teaspoons baking powder

For the filling:
200g/7 oz mascarpone
100g/3 ½ oz chocolate spread

For the icing:
300ml/10 ½ fl oz double (heavy) cream
2 tablespoons chocolate spread

For the decoration:
150g/5 ¼ oz dark chocolate

Method
Cut baking parchment discs for the bases of 2 x20cm round sandwich tins. Butter the tins and lay the papers in. Preheat the oven to 180C/350F/Gas 4.

Break the chocolate for the cake into a heat proof bowl and set over a saucepan on a medium-low heat (the bowl should not touch the water). Once melted, set aside until cool, but not set. Mix the coffee with 2 tablespoons of boiling water and set aside to cool.

Put the butter and sugar into a bowl and beat with an electric whisk until light and creamy. Thoroughly beat in each egg, one by one. If the mixture starts to split, add 1 tablespoon of the flour to bring it back.

Sift in the rest of the flour, the cocoa powder and baking powder, then fold them in. Pour in the melted chocolate and coffee and fold in. Divide the batter between the prepared tins, smooth it out and bake for 18-20 minutes.

Meanwhile, mix the mascarpone with the chocolate spread until smooth and well blended.

Melt the 150g/5 ¼ oz of plain chocolate and spread it onto a large baking sheet covered with baking parchment (we used two medium size baking sheets). Spread it over in a fairly thin layer, thin enough to look good but not too thin so that it breaks when set. Place in the fridge until ready.

Whip the double cream until thick then mix in the chocolate spread so that it is a piping consistency.

Check that the cakes are cooked by poking a cocktail stick into the centre; if it comes out clean then it's cooked; if it's got cake mix on it, give it another 2 minutes before testing it again. Take out and set on a wire rack. Once cool enough to touch, pop them out of the tins and return to the rack to fully cool.

Spread a layer of frosting on the bottom layer, then gently press the top layer on, spread a thin layer of the frosting around the edges of the cake (so that the chocolate has something to stick it to the cake).

Break up the set chocolate into shards and stick around the edge of the cake.

Then pipe the whipped chocolate cream onto the top of the cake.

Orange and cardamom hot chocolate

One of my favourite flavour combinations.

Ingredients
113g/4 oz milk or white chocolate, chopped
500ml/1-pint milk
The seeds from 3 cardamom pods, crushed
1 two-inch strip of orange zest
½ teaspoon vanilla extract

Method
Pop the milk into a saucepan over a low heat and add in the cardamom seeds and the orange zest, heat until the milk is just below boiling.

Put the chocolate into a bowl and strain the milk over the top, stir the milk and chocolate until the chocolate dissolves adding in the vanilla extract.

Serve topped with whipped cream and a sprinkle of cinnamon if you like.

A short cut is to use orange flavoured chocolate then you won't need to add the orange zest.

July

Chicken, leek and corn soup
Sausage and stuffing pie
Mushroom pie
Vegetable moussaka
Herb bread
Soft pretzels
Savoury scones
Summer pudding
Flapjack / oat cookie slice
Orange sponge cake
Hokey pokey cookies
Chocolate brownie meringue cake
Vanilla cream puffs
Mocha hot chocolate

The centre of summer. The birds are singing, the bees are buzzing, the butterflies are flittering. Mother Nature is at her height producing amazing produce for us to eat. This is a good month to have picnics and eat supper outside in the evening.

This is a basic list of produce that is usually in season during the month of July. It will obviously vary depending on where you are in the world and what the weather has been like. Be guided by what you find in your local greengrocers or farmers market. If you shop in the supermarket, check for labels that say it is 'new season'.

Aubergine/eggplant, beetroot, broad beans, broccoli, cabbage (green), carrots, cauliflower, chives, courgette/zucchinis, cucumber, fennel, French beans, garlic, lettuce, onions, peas, peppers & chillies, potatoes, radish, runner beans, spinach, sweetcorn, tomatoes.

Apricots, blackberries, blackcurrants, blueberries, cherries, gooseberries, melon, peaches, nectarines, raspberries, redcurrants, outdoor rhubarb, strawberries, white currants (UK).

Apricots, blackberries, blueberries, melon, kiwi, mangoes, peaches, plums, raspberries, strawberries (USA).

Chicken, leek and corn soup

This soup is delicious and a big family favourite. It can also be made vegetarian if you prefer.

Ingredients
1 large tin sweetcorn or 2 large corn cobs
2 tablespoons vegetable oil
6 bacon rashers, diced
1 onion, chopped
1 clove garlic, crushed
2 large potatoes, diced
1 large chicken breast or the meat from 4 chicken thighs, skinned and diced
1 litre/35 fl oz chicken or vegetable stock
1 tablespoon chopped fresh chives
Salt and pepper

Method
Cut the kernels from the corn cobs with a sharp knife (or open the tin). Heat the oil in a pan and add the bacon, onion and garlic. Fry for about ten minutes but keep it on a low heat as you don't want it to brown. Add the potatoes, chicken and corn along with the stock. Simmer for about twenty minutes until the potatoes are tender and the chicken is cooked.

Season with salt and pepper, sprinkle over the chives and serve.

Options
To make this vegetarian leave out the chicken and bacon and replace with butter beans and sliced mushrooms.

Swirl in a few tablespoons of cream to give it a rich flavour.

Sausage and stuffing pie

This is lovely to eat hot with baked potatoes or salad but works equally well cold to take on a picnic.

Ingredients
800g/2 lbs sausages with the skins removed or plain sausage meat
125g/ 4 ½ oz breadcrumbs
3 tablespoons chopped herbs (mixture of parsley, sage and thyme works well)
6 tablespoons chutney (caramelised onion chutney is good)
1 tablespoon milk

For the pastry:
125g/4 ½ oz plain (all purpose) flour
55g/2 oz butter, cubed
30-45ml/2-3 tbsp cold water

Method
Rub the butter into the flour until it resembles breadcrumbs then slowly stir in the water a little at a time until it comes together as a dough.

Pre-heat the oven to 190C/375F/Gas 5.

Divide the pastry in two, one half slightly bigger than the other. Roll out the small piece into a rectangle and place it on a baking tray lined with a piece of parchment paper.

Mix the sausage meat in a bowl with the breadcrumbs, herbs and chutney. Lay this mixture on to the pastry base in a line down the centre. Roll out the larger piece of pastry and lay it over the sausage mixture. Wet the pastry edges and seal them together, crimping them over as you go. Basically, you are making a huge sausage roll. With a sharp knife score a few air holes in the top of the pie. Brush with milk.

Pop in the oven for about forty minutes, until it is golden brown.

Options
Swap the caramelised onion chutney for pickle or tomato chutney or mango chutney.

Mushroom pie (vegan option)

I am not a big fan of mushrooms, but I must admit this pie is totally lovely!

Ingredients
Vegetable oil
250g/9 oz mushrooms, chopped
1 large onion, diced
1 tablespoon balsamic vinegar
2 tablespoons plain flour (all purpose)
200ml/7 fl oz milk (I use almond milk)
1 vegetable stock cube
Salt and pepper

Pastry:
200g/7 oz wholemeal flour
100g/3 ½ oz margarine or butter (vegan margarine works well)
1 teaspoon dried parsley

Method
Preheat your oven to 200C/400F/Gas 6.

To make the filling heat a couple of tablespoons of vegetable oil in a large pan, add the mushrooms and onion and fry on a low heat for about ten minutes, until golden. Remove the onions and mushrooms and set aside. Using the same frying pan, mix in the two tablespoons of plain flour. Crumble the stock cube into the saucepan and gradually whisk in the milk. Add the vinegar and season with salt and pepper. Add the onions and mushrooms back in. Simmer on a low heat for a couple of minutes.

To make the pastry pop the flour, thyme and margarine into a bowl and season with salt and pepper. Rub the fat into the flour until it resembles breadcrumbs. Gradually add in 4-6 teaspoons of cold water, a little at a time until you get a crumbly dough. Roll out the pastry.

Spoon the mushroom filling into a pie dish and top with a pastry lid, seal the edges. Glaze with a little milk. Make a small hole in the centre of the pie lid with a knife. Bake for 40 minutes, until golden brown.

Vegetable moussaka (vegan option)

This makes a big dish that would serve 10 or 12. The preparation takes a bit of time, but it is worth the effort. If you are cooking for a party, you can make and bake it the day before and just warm it up when you need it. If you want to make this dish vegan, you can leave out the béchamel sauce and top with grated vegan cheese.

Ingredients
3 medium courgettes (zucchini), sliced thinly
3 large potatoes, peeled and sliced thinly
2 small aubergines (eggplant)
2 cloves garlic, peeled
1 large onion, diced
280g/10 oz cooked lentils (I like to use puy lentils as they hold their shape)
1 large red pepper (bell), sliced
2 cans tinned chopped tomatoes
3 tablespoons fresh dill, chopped
1 teaspoon dried oregano
½ teaspoon ground cinnamon
½ teaspoon cayenne pepper
150g/5 ¼ oz feta cheese (crumbled)
10 tablespoons grated parmesan cheese
55g/2 oz butter
3 tablespoons flour (white or gluten free)
750ml/26 ½ fl oz milk (cow's or soya)
1 large egg, beaten
¼ teaspoon ground nutmeg
Olive oil
Salt and pepper

Method

Preheat your oven to 400F/220C/Gas 6. Grease two baking sheets with olive oil and spread the courgette, potatoes and garlic cloves in a single layer across them. Brush the tops of the vegetables with some more olive oil and sprinkle with salt and pepper. Pop them in the oven and roast for ten minutes, then swap the racks around and roast for a further 10 minutes until they are tender and starting to turn golden brown. Remove from the oven and set aside. Crush the roasted garlic cloves ready for use later.

Cut the aubergine into slices, re-grease the baking sheets with olive oil and spread the aubergine slices across them. Sprinkle with salt and pepper. Bake in the oven for 10-15 minutes until the slices are tender and lightly golden.

Meanwhile heat two tablespoons olive oil in a large pan over a medium heat. Sauté the onion until soft, add the pepper slices and the roasted garlic and cook for a couple of minutes more. Add in the cooked lentils, diced tomatoes, fresh dill, oregano, cinnamon, cayenne pepper and a dash of salt. Stir and then reduce the heat slightly and cook for about five minutes until warmed through.

When the aubergine is cooked remove it from the oven and reduce the oven temperature to 375F/190C/Gas 5.

Lightly grease a large baking pan/dish. Place a single layer of the roasted aubergine slices on the bottom of the dish. On top of that place a layer of potatoes and courgettes. Spread the lentil mixture evenly in a single layer over the surface.

Sprinkle with two tablespoons of grated parmesan and ½ cup crumbled feta on top of the lentil mixture. Place the remaining sliced potatoes and courgettes on top of the cheese.

Finish with a layer of aubergine and sprinkle two more tablespoons of grated parmesan on top.

Place the dish in the oven for 20 minutes. Whilst the moussaka is baking make the béchamel sauce. In a pan melt the butter and whisk the flour into the melted butter until it is dissolved and thick. Continue whisking for a couple of minutes until the mixture turns a light sandy brown colour. Slowly whisk in the milk. Bring the mixture to a simmer then reduce the heat slightly. Whisk in two tablespoons grated parmesan cheese. Continue whisking for a couple of minutes until the sauce starts to thicken. Remove from the heat and mix in a dash of salt, nutmeg and black pepper to taste. Whisk the beaten egg slowly into the sauce.

Remove the moussaka from the oven and pour the sauce evenly over the top. Sprinkle ¼ cup parmesan cheese over the top. Bake for a further 30 minutes until the top is golden brown.

Herb bread

This lovely loaf incorporates the summer bounty of fresh herbs.

Ingredients
500g/1 lb self-raising flour
1 teaspoon dry mustard powder
2 tablespoons chopped herbs (chives, sage, parsley, basil, thyme)
100g/3 ½ oz cheddar cheese, grated
25g/0.8 oz butter
1 egg, beaten
150ml/5 fl oz water

Method
Preheat the oven to 375F/190C/Gas 5. Grease a 2lb loaf tin.

Mix together the flour, mustard, herbs and cheese.

Melt the butter and add it to the flour mixture. Pop in the egg and water a mix to a soft dough. It will look slightly wet and cake batter like. Turn into the loaf tin and bake for about an hour. It should be well risen and golden brown.

Soft pretzels

These pretzels are so easy to make and absolutely delicious whether you dip them in a cheese sauce or a chocolate one. If you are creative, they can be made into all sorts of different shapes; crescent moons, Celtic knots, plaits or even a pentagram. The salt sprinkling on the top brings heap loads of protective energy and the pretzels also make brilliant food offerings to the gods.

Ingredients
340ml/11.5 fl oz warm water
1 tablespoon sugar
2 teaspoons sea salt
1 packet 7g/2 teaspoons active dry yeast
600g/21 oz plain (all-purpose) flour
55g/2 oz butter, melted
Tablespoon of vegetable oil for greasing
1 ½ litres/80 fl oz water
80g/2 ¾ oz bicarbonate soda
1 large egg yolk beaten with 1 tablespoon water

Method
Combine the warm water, sugar and salt in the bowl of a stand mixer and sprinkle the yeast on top. Allow to sit for 5 minutes or until the mixture begins to foam.

Add the flour and butter then using the dough hook attachment mix on a low speed until well combined. Change to medium speed and knead until the dough is smooth and pulls away from the side of the bowl, approximately 4 to 5 minutes. Remove the dough from the bowl, clean the bowl and then oil it well with the vegetable oil. Return the dough to the bowl, cover with plastic wrap and sit in a warm place for approximately 50 to 55 minutes or until the dough has doubled in size.

Preheat the oven to 450F/230C/Gas 8. Line 2 baking sheets with parchment paper and lightly brush with the vegetable oil. Set aside.

Bring the water and the bicarbonate soda to a rolling boil in a large saucepan or roasting pan.

In the meantime, turn the dough out onto a lightly oiled work surface and divide into 8 equal pieces. Roll out each piece of dough and create your pretzel masterpiece. Place onto the parchment-lined baking sheet.

Place the pretzels into the boiling water, one by one, each for 30 seconds. Remove them from the water using a large flat spatula. Return to the baking sheet, brush the top of each pretzel with the beaten egg yolk and water mixture and sprinkle with salt.

Bake until dark golden brown in colour which should take approximately 12 to 14 minutes. Transfer to a cooling rack for at least 5 minutes before serving.

Savoury scones (vegan option)

We love a good scone in our house, although we always argue about how to pronounce it...these are excellent to serve with soup or just for a snack. I have given the basic recipe and then added various options.

Ingredients
225g/8 oz self-raising flour
1 teaspoon baking powder
50g/1 ¾ oz margarine (vegan option)
5 or 6 tablespoons milk (any kind)
Salt and pepper

Method
Preheat your oven to 425F/220C/Gas 7.

Rub the margarine into the flour and baking powder. Add the salt and pepper to taste. Stir in the milk, one tablespoon at a time until you get a soft dough. Roll out onto a floured surface. Keep the dough quite thick, 1-1 /2" (3-4cm). Cut out rounds and pop them onto a baking sheet. You can brush the top with milk if you wish.

Bake in the oven for 12-15 minutes.

Options
Marmite scones - add 1 tablespoon marmite to the mixture.
Mustard scones - add 1 teaspoon mustard powder and ½ teaspoon paprika to the mixture.
Herb scones - add 2 teaspoons mixed herbs or oregano to the mixture.
Cheese scones - add 100g/3 ½ oz grated cheese to the mixture.

Summer pudding

This is a celebration of all the abundance of summer fruits and is really easy to make and can also be made ahead of time.

Ingredients
1 ¼ kg/2 lb 120 oz mixed berries and currants (strawberries, blackberries, redcurrants, raspberries)
175g/6 oz sugar
7 slices white bread, preferably a day old (i.e. not freshly baked)

Method
Put the sugar and 3 tablespoons water into a large pan. Gently heat until the sugar dissolves. Now pop your fruit into the pan - except strawberries. Cook for a few minutes until the fruit starts to soften, not too long - you don't want mush! Now drain the fruit through a sieve but save the juice.

Line a pudding basin with cling wrap, leaving some overhang.

Cut the crusts off the bread. Slice four of the pieces of bread in half on an angle. Cut two slices into four triangles each and leave the last piece whole. This is a bit of a jigsaw.

Dip each slice of bread into the fruit juice just to coat. Line the base and the sides with the cut slices of bread.

Now spoon in the fruit (adding the strawberries if using). Save any left-over juice for serving.

Once full pop the whole slice of bread on the top after dipping in the juice. Trim any overhang.

Pull the cling wrap up and over the top of the pudding. Put a plate over the top and weight it down with weights or tin cans. Chill for at least six hours, preferably overnight.

To serve, open the cling film and pop a serving plate over the basin. Flip it over so that the pudding comes out of the basin and onto the plate. Pour over any juice you had left over.

Flapjack /oat cookie slice

I struggled for a long time to find a flapjack recipe that I liked and one that set properly and didn't leave me with a crumbly or gooey mess...I have finally found it...and the beauty of flapjacks is that you can vary the recipe by adding in different spices.

And for our friends over the pond - we call it a flapjack which I believe is a pancake for you! This is an oaty cookie slice...

Ingredients
100g/3 ½ oz golden syrup
100g/3 ½ oz demerara sugar
125g/4 ½ oz butter, diced
250g/9 oz porridge oats
75g/2 ½ oz mixed seeds (pumpkin, sunflower, sesame)
¼ teaspoon ground ginger
Pinch of salt

Method
Preheat the oven to 180C/350F/Gas 4 and line the base and sides of a 20cm (8") square baking tin with baking parchment.

Pop the golden syrup, sugar and butter into a pan and heat gently until the butter and sugar have dissolved.

Mix the oats, seeds, spice and salt in a large bowl and stir in the melted butter mixture. Stir well.

Spoon into the prepared tin and level the top.

Bake in the middle of the oven for 20-25 minutes. 20 minutes for chewy flapjacks, 25 for crisper ones. The flapjacks will firm up as they cool.

Remove from the oven and mark the flapjack into squares, leave them in the tin to cool completely.

Options

Replace the seeds with finely chopped nuts.

Replace the seeds with dried fruit such as sultanas or chopped dried apricots.

Substitute the ground ginger for ground cinnamon or mixed spice.

Orange sponge cake (vegan)

This makes an incredibly fabulous sponge cake and flavoured with the fresh summery taste of oranges.

Ingredients
100g/3 ½ oz apple puree
200ml/7 fl oz soya or almond milk
80ml/3 fl oz vegetable oil
1 tablespoon cider vinegar
300g/10 ½ oz self-raising flour
½ teaspoon baking powder
165g/6 oz sugar
½ teaspoon salt
Zest of 2 oranges

Filling:
40g/1 ½ oz margarine
100g/3 ½ oz icing sugar (powdered sugar)
2 tablespoons marmalade

Topping:
4 tablespoons icing sugar (powdered sugar)
Orange juice to mix

Method
Preheat the oven to 325F/170C/Gas 3.

Grease two 9" round cake tins and line the base with baking parchment.

Blitz the apple puree until smooth.

Add the oil, vinegar and orange zest to the soya milk, stir and leave to curdle.

Pop the flour, baking powder, sugar and salt into a large bowl. Stir. Add the apple puree to the wet ingredients and stir. Now pour the wet ingredients into the dry and fold very gently. Don't over mix.

Pour the batter between the two tins. Bake in the oven for half an hour, until golden.

Leave to cool in the tins for a couple of minutes then turn out to cool.

To make the filling whisk the margarine and icing sugar together until light and fluffy. Stir the marmalade in. Pipe or spread on the bottom layer of sponge and then pop the other sponge on top.

For the topping stir a teaspoon of orange juice at a time into the icing sugar. Add it slowly, you won't need much. You are looking for a thick pouring consistency. Pour onto the top of the sponge and allow it flow over the surface.

Options
Substitute the orange with lemon or lime.

Hokey pokey cookies (vegan option)

Fabulous name for fabulous cookies.

Ingredients
60g/2 oz butter (vegan option)
115g/4 oz golden syrup
60g/2 oz brown sugar
225g/8 oz self-raising flour

Method
Preheat your oven to 350F/180C/Gas 4.

Line two baking sheets with baking parchment.

Melt the butter, golden syrup and sugar together in a pan over a low heat, stir until the sugar has dissolved. Allow to cool slightly.

Sift the flour into the liquid and stir until it comes together as a dough.

Form tablespoon size balls and place onto the baking sheets.

Press each one down lightly with a fork.

Bake for 10 minutes until just golden.

Leave on the tray for a few minutes before you transfer to a rack to cool.

Chocolate brownie meringue cake

Complete chocolate and sugar overload...

Ingredients
4 egg whites
250g/9 oz caster sugar
Large tub double (heavy cream)
½ teaspoon vanilla extract
Chocolate buttons, chocolate sweets
Chocolate brownies (see recipe below)

Method
Preheat the oven to 140C/275F/Gas 1.

Draw two 8-inch circles on two sheets of baking parchment and place on two baking trays.

Whisk the egg whites until stiff then add in the sugar gradually one spoonful at a time whisking continuously until the mixture is stiff and glossy. Pipe the meringue in a spiral inside the marked circles on the baking parchment to create to 8inch spirals.

Bake the meringue rounds in the oven for 1-1 ¼ hours until crisp and dry. Leave to cool then carefully peel away the baking parchment.

Whip the double cream with the vanilla extract until thick.

Lay one of the meringue discs onto a serving plate and spread or pipe half the double cream over.

Sprinkle with chopped chocolate brownies, chopped chocolate pieces, chocolate buttons or whatever chocolate sweets you like over the cream you can even drizzle some melted chocolate over. Place the second meringue disc on top. Pipe or spoon the remaining whipped cream on top. Decorate with more chopped chocolate brownies and chocolate sweets.

You can use shop bought chocolate brownies as you will only

need two or three, or use this recipe and have some left over to scoff.

Ingredients
200g/7 oz dark chocolate, roughly chopped
175g/6 oz butter
325g/11 ½ oz sugar
130g/4 ½ oz plain (all purpose) flour
3 eggs

Preheat the oven to 170C/325F/Gas 3.

Put the chocolate and butter in a bowl over a saucepan of simmering water until melted and smooth (or use the microwave). Add the sugar into the chocolate mixture and stir well. Add in the flour and stir until incorporated. Then stir in the eggs and mix until thick and smooth.

Pour into a lined 33 x 23cm baking tin.

Bake for 35-45 minutes, the top of the brownie should look flaky but will still be slightly soft in the centre.

Leave to cool completely before slicing.

Vanilla cream puffs

These are made with choux pastry (think profiteroles or eclairs). It often scares people but if you follow the steps it really does work well.

Ingredients

For the choux pastry:
115g/4 oz plain flour (all purpose)
Pinch of salt
115g/4 oz butter, diced
300ml/10 ½ fl oz water
4 eggs, beaten

For the filling:
Large tub of double or whipping cream
Teaspoon vanilla extract
Two tablespoons sugar
Icing sugar (powdered sugar) to dust

Method
Preheat the oven to 200C/400F/gas 6.

Oil a non-stick baking sheet.

Sift the flour and salt into a bowl.

Put the butter and water in a saucepan and bring to the boil, as soon as the butter has melted take the pan off the heat and tip in the flour.

Beat vigorously with a wooden spoon for a couple of minutes over a low heat until the mixture is smooth and glossy and comes away from the sides of the pan.

Remove from the heat and add in the eggs a little a time, beating after each addition. Once the eggs have all been beaten in the dough should be smooth and glossy.

Put spoonfuls of the mixture onto the baking sheet (you should get about 20 puffs out of this mixture) space them apart as they will grow. Bake for 25 minutes or until dry and crisp.

Take them out of the oven and very quickly stick a skewer into each one to allow the steam to escape, put them straight back into the oven for five minutes (with the heat switched off), leaving the oven door open slightly.

Cool on a wire rack.

For the filling, whisk the double cream until stiff and then fold in the essence and sugar.

Pop the cream into a piping bag.

Using the small hole in each puff, fill with cream.

Dust the top with icing sugar.

Options

Stir in spoonfuls of caramel sauce to the whipped cream.

Top the buns with melted chocolate.

Add a teaspoon of ground cinnamon to the cream.

Add a couple of drops of peppermint, orange or rose essence to the cream.

Mocha hot chocolate

Can't decide between hot chocolate or coffee? Then this is the best of both...

Ingredients
500ml/1-pint milk
3 tablespoons sugar
1 tablespoon brown sugar
4 squares of milk or dark chocolate
1 tablespoon instant coffee granules

Method
Place all the ingredients into a saucepan over a low heat and stir continuously until it is heated through and all incorporated.

Serve topped with whipped cream and maybe a drizzle of chocolate syrup.

August

Pumpkin and coconut soup
Spaghetti Bolognese
Holy guca-pastaroni
Gigantes plaki
Greek salad
Rosemary focaccia bread
Ciabatta
Lemon trifle
Caramel swirl cake
Coconut cupcakes
Sunflower cookies
Malteser cake
Vegan hot chocolate

This is the time when our ancestors would have celebrated the first harvest and when the plants start sending out their seeds to reproduce. On the pagan calendar, this festival is often called Lughnasadh. When I think about this time of the year in my head it is filled with fields of grain ready for harvest, birds singing, the sun shining and all feels right with the world, but as I live in the UK the weather isn't always that reliable. The earth starts to prepare itself for the coming autumn but don't dismay as it is a time to celebrate the abundance of the fruits and grains of the harvest and indeed of life itself.

Breads of all kinds feature strongly in the food theme for this celebration along with any kind of grains washed down with a nice homemade wine or cider then round off the meal with local fresh fruits and berries.

This is a basic list of produce that is usually in season during the month of August. It will obviously vary depending on where you are in the world and what the weather has been like. Be guided by what you find in your local greengrocers or farmers market. If you shop in the supermarket, check for labels that say it is 'new season'.

Aubergine/eggplants, beetroot, broad beans, broccoli, cabbage (green), carrots, cauliflower, chives, courgette/zucchinis, cucumber, fennel, French beans, garlic, leeks, lettuce, onions, peas, peppers & chillies, potatoes, pumpkins & squashes, radish, runner beans, spinach, sweetcorn, tomatoes.

Apples, apricots, blackberries, blackcurrants, blueberries, cherries, gooseberries, melon, peaches, nectarines, pears, plums, raspberries, outdoor rhubarb, strawberries, white currants (UK).

Apples, apricots, blueberries, melon, figs, kiwi, mangoes, peaches, plums, raspberries (USA).

Pumpkin and coconut soup

This soup just shouts summer sunshine!

Ingredients
1 small pumpkin, peeled and diced
2 large sweet potatoes, peeled and diced
1 litre/35 fl oz vegetable stock
2 leeks, chopped
1 chilli, diced
2" piece of root ginger, peeled and grated
3 cloves garlic, crushed
Salt and pepper
2 large handfuls of greens or cabbage, sliced thinly
1 can (14 oz) coconut milk
Squeeze of lime juice
½ teaspoon dried thyme or 1 teaspoon fresh thyme

Method
Pop the stock in a pan and add the squash and sweet potato, cook for about twenty minutes then add in the leeks, chilli, ginger and garlic. Season with salt and pepper. Cook for a further half an hour. Add in the greens/cabbage and simmer for about 20 minutes.

Stir in the coconut milk, lime and thyme.

Cook for about five minutes then serve.

Options
Replace the pumpkin with butternut squash, in fact most squashes work well in this recipe.

Replace the sweet potatoes with carrots.

Ramp up the heat by using two chillies instead of just one.

Replace the greens with sliced bell peppers.

Add in a handful of cooked, shreddedchicken before serving.

Spaghetti bolognese

We have probably all got our own family versions of this classic dish, this is ours. Serve it with spaghetti. If you have left overs the Bolognese is excellent served over baked potatoes. Although my daughter likes to have it cold...in a sandwich.

Ingredients
750g/ 1 ½ lb mince - you can use all beef mince, but I like to use half beef and half lamb
1 pack of bacon rashers, chopped
1 large onion, diced
3 cloves garlic, crushed
2 large carrots, diced
3 bell peppers, diced
1 courgette (zucchini), diced
2 tablespoons oregano
1 tablespoon basil
1 tablespoon Worcestershire sauce
1 teaspoon sugar
2 tablespoons tomato puree
2 beef stock cubes
1 tin chopped tomatoes (400g)
1 jar tomato passata (500g)
1 tablespoon plain (all purpose) flour
Salt and pepper

Method
Fry the bacon and mince in a large pan. Add the chopped onion and crushed garlic. Sauté for a few minutes then add in the carrots, peppers and courgettes. Cook for a further five minutes then add the herbs, Worcestershire sauce, sugar, tomato puree, chopped tomatoes, tomato passata and the flour. Crumble in the stock cubes and season with salt and

pepper. Stir it all together. If it seems a little dry add a dash of water.

You can either leave it to simmer away on a low heat on top of the stove for about forty minutes. However, I like to pop it in the oven and slow cook for a couple of hours on 180C/350F/ Gas 4.

Options

Make a vegetarian/vegan version by replacing the meat with 3 sweet potatoes or 1 butternut squash, diced.

Holy guca-pastaroni

A funky twist on a pasta salad that can be eaten hot or cold. This is also a vegan recipe (if you don't add the optional tuna).

Ingredients
400g/14 oz pasta shapes
Salt and pepper
3 ripe avocados
3 tablespoons lime juice
2 tablespoons olive oil
4 spring onions
20 cherry tomatoes or 6 large tomatoes
Handful fresh parsley
1 tin tuna (optional)

Method
Cook the pasta in boiling salted water until al dente.

Halve the avocados, remove the stones and scoop the flesh out into a bowl. Sprinkle with the lime juice and the olive oil. Mix and season to taste with salt and pepper. Roughly mash the avocado mixture with a fork. You don't want it smooth, just crushed. Slice the spring onions and chop the tomatoes and the parsley. Add these to the avocado and mix together.

Drain the pasta and tip it into the avocado mixture, stir well.

If you want you can add in a tin of tuna, stir together.

Options
Throw in chopped boiled eggs.
Add chopped ham or cooked chicken instead of the tuna.
Bulk it out with a tin of cooked mixed beans instead of tuna.

Gigantes plaki (giant beans) (vegan)

This is a lovely side dish or even a main dish that is super simple to make and also happens to be vegan as well.

Ingredients
A tin of cooked butter beans
3 tablespoons olive oil
1 large onion, finely chopped
2 garlic cloves, finely chopped
2 tablespoons tomato puree
2 tins chopped tomatoes
1 teaspoon sugar
1 teaspoon dried oregano
Pinch ground cinnamon
2 tablespoons chopped parsley

Method
Heat the oven to 180C/160C/Gas 4. Heat the olive oil in a large pan and sauté the onion and garlic over a medium heat for about ten minutes until soft. Add the tomato puree and cook for another minute. Add in the remaining ingredients and simmer for a couple of minutes. Season with salt and pepper and tip into a large ovenproof dish. Bake for about an hour uncovered. Once cool sprinkle the parsley over the top.

Greek salad

A simple salad but packed full of flavour.

Ingredients
4 large tomatoes sliced into wedges

1 cucumber, chopped

½ red onion, thinly sliced

16 olives

1 teaspoon dried oregano

3 tablespoons feta cheese cut into chunks

4 tablespoons olive oil

Method
Throw it all in a bowl, season and mix together.

Rosemary focaccia bread

This is another firm family favourite; with the rosemary and salt it is delicious and never lasts long.

Ingredients
500g/1 lb strong white bread flour
1 teaspoon salt
7g/2 teaspoons dried fast action yeast (1 sachet)
3 tablespoons olive oil
300ml/10 ½ fl oz warm water
A few sprigs fresh rosemary, chopped
Olive oil, rosemary sprigs and sea salt to drizzle

Method
Pop the flour into a large bowl and add the salt and rosemary. Stir in the dried yeast.

Pour the olive oil in along with the warm lukewarm water and mix together. The dough will be slightly sticky, a wet dough makes a good focaccia!

If the dough appears dry, add a dash more water.

Oil a board with a little olive oil and turn the dough out. Knead for about ten minutes (5 minutes if you use a mixer with a dough hook).

Pop the dough back in the bowl, cover and leave in a warm place for an hour to 1 ½ hours, until doubled in size.

Grease a baking tin (approx. 20cm x 30cm) with olive oil.

Turn out the dough and very gently press it into the baking tin. Try not to handle it too much but lightly push the dough into the rectangle shape of the tin, it doesn't need to be perfect.

Now push your finger into the dough at regular intervals to make dimples. Tuck a few bits of rosemary into the indentations.

Cover and leave to rise for a further hour.

Preheat the oven to 425F/220C/Gas 7.

Uncover the dough and drizzle over some olive oil and give it a sprinkle of sea salt.

Bake for about 25 minutes until it is a lovely golden brown. Turn out of the tin as soon as it is out of the oven. It doesn't keep very well so I advise eating it warm on the day of baking (it shouldn't be too much of a problem…).

Ciabatta

Another family favourite, this is a wet dough, and can be tricky to work with, but keep with it.

Ingredients
500g/1 lb strong white bread flour, plus extra for dusting
Heaped teaspoon salt
10g/1 ½ teaspoons instant yeast
40ml/1 ¼ fl oz olive oil
400ml/14 fl oz tepid water

Method
Lightly oil a 2-3 litre square plastic container. (It's important to use a square tub as it helps shape the dough).

Put the flour into a bowl and add the salt on one side and the yeast on the other side. Add the olive oil and ¾ of the water and mix. As the dough starts to come together slowly add the rest of the water. Knead for ten minutes. The dough will be quite wet - this makes for a good ciabatta. Tip the dough into the prepared tub, cover and leave to prove until doubled in size, about an hour, but no more than two hours.

Preheat your oven to 425F/220C/Gas 7. Line two baking trays with parchment.

Tip the dough onto a floured surface, trying to keep them as square as possible. Very gently cut the dough in half lengthways and then in half again so that you have 4 equal rectangles of dough. Stretch it length ways a little and place onto the prepared trays. This is a bit tricky, just be gentle and you will get there!

Leave the dough to rest for ten minutes then bake for 25 minutes, until golden brown.

Lemon trifle

This is a variation on the more traditional trifle. What goes into a trifle is much debated - should there be jelly or not? This one is rather a simple, but posh, grown up version.

Ingredients
100g/3 ½ oz sponge fingers or madeira cake
100g/3 ½ oz lemon curd
3 tablespoons liqueur - limoncello works well
500ml/1-pint double (heavy) cream
250ml/9 fl oz double (heavy) cream to decorate
120g/4 ¼ oz sugar
100ml/3 ½ fl oz lemon juice

Method
Slice the sponge fingers in half or cut the madeira cake into slices, spread each one with lemon curd. Put them in the base of a large serving dish. Sprinkle the liqueur over the sponge.

Pour 500ml/1-pint cream into a pan and add the sugar, bring to the boil slowly then turn down to a simmer for two or three minutes. Remove from the heat and stir in the lemon juice. Pour this over the sponge.

Leave to cool, then pop in the fridge for a couple of hours until the mixture has set.

Whip the 250ml/9 fl oz of cream until soft, but thick. Spoon the cream over the trifle.

Caramel swirl cake

My husband declared this *"the best cake you have ever made"*...
need I say more?

Ingredients

For the cake batter:
450g/15 ¾ oz plain (all purpose) flour
4 teaspoons baking powder
½ teaspoon salt
200g/7 oz sugar
350ml/12 fl oz milk
2 teaspoons vanilla extract
2 eggs
100g/3 ½ oz butter, melted

Topping mix:
200g/7 oz brown sugar
2 tablespoons flour
200g/7 oz butter, very soft (almost to point of melted)

Sweet glaze:
300g/10 ½ oz icing/powdered sugar
5 tablespoons milk
1 teaspoon vanilla extract

Method
Preheat oven to 350F/180C/Gas 4.

In a large mixing bowl combine together all "batter" ingredients
except for butter.

Once mixed, slowly add in the butter and combine.

Pour into a greased 9"x13" baking pan.

Mix together all ingredients for topping mix until well combined.

Pour over cake batter and swirl with a knife.

Bake for 35-45 until fully baked.

Mix together all the sweet glaze ingredients, set aside until cake is done.

Once cake is done, remove from oven, and while still warm drizzle glaze over cake.

Coconut cupcakes (vegan)

These are totally lush and because the frosting is made with coconut oil and not butter/margarine they aren't too sickly either…you can eat lots!

Ingredients
270g/9 ½ oz plain (all-purpose flour)
200g/7 oz sugar
1 teaspoon baking powder
1 teaspoon bicarbonate soda
½ teaspoon salt
220g/7 ¾ oz coconut milk
90g/3 oz vegetable oil
2 teaspoons vanilla extract
1 tablespoon cider vinegar

Frosting:
200g/7 oz coconut oil (solid, room temperature)
360g/12 ½ oz icing sugar (powdered sugar)
1 teaspoon vanilla extract
2 tablespoons coconut or soya milk
4 tablespoons desiccated coconut
Flaked coconut for decoration

Method
Preheat the oven to 350F/180C/Gas 4.

Line two cupcake trays with paper cases, you should get 14-16 from this recipe.

Mix together the flour, sugar, baking powder, bicarbonate of soda and salt. In a separate bowl whisk together the coconut milk, oil, vanilla and vinegar. Pour the wet ingredients into the dry and whisk until combined. Be careful not to over mix.

Fill the cupcake cases about two thirds full. Bake in the oven for about 15 minutes, until a skewer inserted into the centre comes out clean. Cool.

To make the frosting; using a mixer beat the coconut oil until smooth. Slowly add the icing sugar until combined then add in the vanilla. Add 1 tablespoon coconut milk and if needed add another. It needs to be a spreadable consistency. Beat for a further five minutes until the frosting is light and fluffy. Stir through the desiccated coconut.

Ice your cupcakes and sprinkle with flaked coconut.

Sunflower cookies (vegan option)

These look like beautiful sunshiny flowers and taste delicious.

Ingredients
450g/15 ¾ oz plain flour (all-purpose flour)
1 teaspoon salt
225g/8 oz butter (vegan option)
4-6 tablespoons cold water
175g/6 oz smooth peanut butter
175g/6 oz sugar
Red food colouring

Method
Preheat the oven to 180C/350F/Gas 4. Grease a baking sheet or put a sheet of baking parchment on top.

Pop the flour into a bowl, add the salt and butter and rub together until they resemble breadcrumbs. Then add the cold water a little at a time and combine until the pastry forms a ball. Roll the dough into a sausage shape and cut into 12 equal slices and roll into balls.

To make the filling mix the peanut butter with the sugar. Flatten the balls of pastry into discs and fill each one with a spoonful of the filling. Seal up the edges turn over and pat flat.

Paint a red dot on the middle of each disc and let the food colouring dry. Then put twelve incisions in the pastries around the edge of the red dot and twist each 'petal' to the right.

Pop them onto the baking tray and bake for 15-20 minutes until golden brown.

Options
If you don't like peanut butter replace it with almond butter.

Malteser cake

This looks incredibly impressive and tastes just as good.

Ingredients
150g/5 ¼ oz butter, softened
250g/9 oz sugar
150g/5 ¼ oz self-raising flour
125g/4 ½ oz sour cream
4 medium eggs
50g/1 ¾ oz cocoa powder
1 teaspoon baking powder
Pinch salt
½ teaspoon vanilla extract
100g/3 ½ oz dark chocolate
550g/19 oz icing sugar (powdered sugar)
250g/9 oz butter, softened
1 tablespoons milk
500g/1 lb Maltesers (chocolate coated malted balls)

Method
Preheat the oven to 180C/350F/Gas 4. Grease two 8-inch sandwich tins and line the bases with baking parchment.

Put the butter, sugar, flour, sour cream, eggs, cocoa powder, baking powder, vanilla extract and salt into a bowl then mix until smooth.

Divide evenly between the two tins and level the tops. Bake in the centre of the oven for 25-30 minutes.

Remove from the oven and leave to cool in the tins for a few minutes before turning out onto a wire rack to cool completely.

To make the butter cream break the chocolate into pieces and microwave carefully (30 second blasts at a time) or in a bowl over a pan of simmering water until melted.

Sift the icing sugar into a bowl, add the butter and milk and beat until it is really light and fluffy. Then pour in the melted chocolate stirring continuously.

Pop one of the cakes onto a serving plate then spread over a third of the butter cream. Sit the other sponge on top and spread the remaining butter cream all over the tops and sides of the complete cake. It doesn't need to be perfect as you are going to cover it with chocolate sweets.

Next you stick the Maltesers all over the cake…this is seriously boring but worth the effort! If you don't like Maltesers you could use chocolate buttons.

Vegan hot chocolate

You can substitute any kind of plant milk for the other hot chocolate recipes in this book, but this one is a good basic vegan recipe.

Ingredients
500ml/1-pint almond or soya milk
3 tablespoons cocoa powder
1 tablespoon sugar

Method
Warm the milk in a saucepan over a low heat until just before boiling.

Mix the cocoa powder and sugar together in a mug, pour the warm milk on top and mix until combined.

You can substitute soya or almond milk to most of the hot chocolate recipes in this book, you can also substitute cocoa powder for cacao if you prefer. Coconut milk also works well, but obviously you get the taste of coconut!

September

Mexican pumpkin soup
Hash it
Baked corn and courgette (zucchini)
Calabacitas
Cheesy parsnip and sweet potato pies
Granary loaf
Indian fry bread
Goddess pudding
Apple sponge cake
Banana choc chip muffins
Fat apple rascals
Apple crumble cake
Butter sugar cookies
Kicking hot chocolate

When we start to wind down in September, produce is still in full abundance. But September hosts the Autumn Equinox which brings about the balance of equal day and night. It is a time to not only celebrate the second harvest of the year but also to give thanks for all that we have, to look back on the warm summer months and all that they have brought us and to welcome the colder, darker days and nights ahead. Bread features again for this celebration along with cake (of course, there always has to be cake), fruits, nuts and vegetables.

This is a basic list of produce that is usually in season during the month of September. It will obviously vary depending on where you are in the world and what the weather has been like. Be guided by what you find in your local greengrocers or farmers market. If you shop in the supermarket, check for labels that say it is 'new season'.

Aubergine/eggplant, beetroot, broad beans, broccoli, cabbage (green), carrots, cauliflower, celery, chives, courgette/ zucchinis, cucumber, fennel, French beans, garlic, leeks, lettuce, onions, parsnip, peas, peppers & chillies, potatoes, pumpkins & squashes, radish, runner beans, spinach, swede, sweetcorn, tomatoes.

Apples, blackberries black currants, blueberries, cherries, damsons, melon, peaches, nectarines, pears, plums, raspberries red currants, outdoor rhubarb, strawberries (UK).

Apples, melon, figs, grapes, mangoes, pomegranates (USA).

Mexican pumpkin soup

Spicy seasonal pumpkin soup - it's a winner!

Ingredients
1 pumpkin or squash, peeled, and diced
3 tablespoons olive or vegetable oil
2 onions, chopped
½ teaspoon paprika
3 garlic cloves, crushed
1 teaspoon dried chilli flakes or 1 large jalapeno, chopped
Tin chopped tomatoes (400g)
1 litre/35 fl oz vegetable stock
Tin of red kidney beans, drained (425g)
Tin of sweet corn or cooked kernels from two large corn cobs
Lime juice
Salt and pepper

Method
Heat the oil in a pan and add the onions and the diced pumpkin, sauté for about five minutes. Stir in the paprika, garlic and chilli. Cook for a further five minutes. Add in the tomatoes, kidney beans, corn and stock, simmer for about 15 minutes. Squeeze in some lime juice and season with salt and pepper.

Options
Serve crushed tortilla chips on the top with a spoonful of sour cream and a few slices of avocado.
Add in two tablespoons chopped coriander.
Sprinkle with grated cheese before serving.
Stir in a handful of cooked, shredded chicken before you serve.
If you like it hot, stir in a tablespoon of chilli sauce.

Hash it

Lunch, dinner or even breakfast if you are hungry. This is an excellent, filling and easy dish to make. I also like to top it with boiled or poached eggs.

Ingredients
2 large potatoes, diced
2 tablespoons vegetable oil
1 large onion or 2 leeks, sliced
200g/7 oz cabbage or Brussel sprouts, sliced
Salt and pepper
6 cooked sausages or a tin of corned beef, cut into chunks

Method
Boil the potatoes in a pan of water until just cooked, drain.

Heat the oil in a frying pan and cook the leeks or onion for five minutes. Add the potatoes, fry for a further five minutes, stir frequently.

Add the sliced cabbage or sprouts and the sausages or corned beef and cook for another five minutes. Season with salt and pepper.

Options
Add in sliced bell peppers.

Throw in a sliced chilli or pinch of chilli flakes.

Stir in two teaspoons of mustard before serving.

To make this vegetarian leave out the sausages or corned beef, to make it vegan don't top with the eggs. Add in some extra vegetables such as peppers or a tin of butter beans to make it more filling.

Baked corn & courgette (zucchini)

This time of year always sees a glut of courgettes (zucchini), this is a lovely recipe to make the most of them.

Ingredients
3 ears of corn or 350g/12 ¼ oz frozen corn kernels
1 medium onion, finely chopped
1 clove garlic, minced
Oil for frying
1 large courgette/zucchini, cubed
1 red or green bell pepper, sliced thinly
1 tin chopped tomatoes (400g)
1 teaspoon chilli powder
Salt and pepper
85g/3 oz grated cheese (cheddar)

Method
If using fresh corn, scrape off the kernels from the cob.
Preheat the oven to 350F/180C/Gas 4.
In a large pan, sauté the onion and garlic in oil for 3-4 minutes. Add the zucchini/courgette and pepper and sauté for a couple more minutes. Add the corn, tomatoes, chilli powder and salt and pepper to taste.
Pour the mixture into a casserole dish and bake covered with foil for fifteen minutes. Remove from the oven and sprinkle the grated cheese over the top, bake for a further ten minutes or until the cheese has melted.

Options
Use mozzarella instead of cheddar. Crush a bag of potato chips and sprinkle on the top before you cover with cheese and bake.
Add in a few rashers of bacon, chopped and fried.
Add a couple of cooked chicken breasts, shredded.

Calabacitas

A mince dish that is easy and simple to make, but very delicious.

Ingredients
900g/2lbs minced beef or pork
Oil to fry
1 large onion, chopped
3 potatoes, peeled and thinly sliced
1 large courgette/zucchini, cubed
2 tomatoes, sliced
1 green chilli, chopped
Salt to taste

Method
Preheat the oven to 325F/170C/Gas 3.

In a large pan sauté, the mince in the oil for about five minutes, until nicely browned.

Add remaining ingredients and simmer for 3-4 minutes.

Tip into a casserole dish, cover with foil and bake for about 40 minutes.

Cheesy parsnip & sweet potato pies

These are gorgeous warm from the oven, but also excellent to take out as a snack for those autumn walks.

Ingredients

For the pastry:
200g/7 oz plain flour (all purpose)
¼ teaspoon salt
½ teaspoon cayenne pepper
100g/3 ½ oz butter, chilled & diced
100g/3 ½ oz mature cheddar cheese, grated
100g/3 ½ oz feta cheese, cubed
3 tablespoons cold water
1 egg for glazing

For the filling:
1 large parsnip, peeled & diced
1 sweet potato, peeled & diced
½ teaspoon dried thyme
Salt & pepper

Method
Pre-heat your oven to 200C/400F/Gas 6.

Pop the parsnip and sweet potato into a pan of boiling water and cook until just done, drain then season with salt and pepper to taste and sprinkle with the thyme and leave aside to cool.

Whilst the veggies are cooking make the pastry. Put the flour, salt and cayenne pepper into a bowl and add in the diced butter. Rub with your fingers until the mixture resembles breadcrumbs or you can pulse it in the food processer (the mixture not your fingers). Stir in the grated cheese. Then slowly add the water mixing together to form a dough. You may need less than 3 tablespoons of water or you might need a drop more to bring it all together.

Cover the dough with cling wrap and pop in the fridge for about 15 minutes to chill.

Roll out the dough on a floured surface and then using cookie cutters (one larger than the other) cut out 8 circles that are large enough to fit into muffin tin holes. Then cut 8 smaller circles to form the lids of the pies.

Spoon the veggie mixture into each pastry bottom until it reaches the top. Put a couple of cubes of feta cheese on top of the mixture then pop the pastry lid onto each one. Press the edges firmly to create a seal. Brush the tops with beaten egg.

Pop into the oven and bake for about 30 minutes until they are golden brown.

Options
You can substitute the parsnip or sweet potato for any root vegetable such as potato or swede and butternut squash works well too.

Granary loaf

I always feel a bit virtuous eating this loaf, it has a 'feel healthy' factor to it, and of course it is tasty too.

Ingredients
500g/1 lb granary bread flour
1 ¼ teaspoons salt
1 ½ teaspoons fast action dried yeast
275ml/9 ½ fl oz warm water
2 teaspoons sugar (optional)

Method

Mix the flour, sugar (if using) and salt together, rub in the butter then stir in the dried yeast. Pour in the water and mix to a soft dough. Knead for about ten minutes (5 minutes in a mixer with a dough hook). Place in a greased 2lb loaf tin or shape into a round and pop on a greased baking sheet. Cover with a tea towel and leave in a warm place for about 1 ½ hours, until doubled in size.

Preheat your oven to 450F/230C/Gas 6.

Uncover and bake the loaf for about half an hour until golden brown.

Indian fry bread

I read about this and had to have a go; it is seriously tasty.

Ingredients
385g/13 ½ oz plain flour (all-purpose flour)
1 tablespoon baking powder
½ teaspoon salt
236ml/8.3 fl oz warm water
Oil for deep frying

Method

Combine flour, baking powder and salt in a large bowl, add the warm water in small amounts and knead the dough until soft but not sticky (I do this in a mixer with a dough hook). You may need more flour or water just add it slowly. Cover the bowl and let stand for about 15 minutes.

Heat oil in your fryer or deep pan. Take large egg size balls of dough and roll out into rounds about ¼" thick, pierce several times with a fork to allow the dough to puff. I make smaller individual ones or larger sharing breads by adjusting the amount of dough I rolled out.

Drop your rolled-out dough into the hot oil one or two at a time, don't over crowd the pan. Cook for about 20 to 30 seconds on each side, turning them over until nicely golden brown.

Goddess pudding

In the UK we have a traditional English dessert called Eve's pudding which is made with apples, I often twist it to use peaches instead, but you could use any kind of fruit. I have renamed it Goddess pudding.

Ingredients
3 or 4 peaches, apricots or apples
100g/3 ½ oz butter
100g/3 ½ oz caster sugar
100g/3 ½ oz self-raising flour
2 eggs
1 teaspoon vanilla extract

Method
Chop the fruit into chunks and lay them on the bottom of a greased ovenproof dish (I used a flan dish).

Cream the butter and caster sugar together. Work in the eggs, sifted flour and vanilla and mix to a soft batter. Spread over the peaches. Bake at 350F/180 C/gas mark 4 for 40 minutes. Serve warm with custard or cream.

Options
Use apples, apricots, peaches or pears.
You could also use cherries or blueberries.
Pop in 1 teaspoon mixed spice to pep up the topping.

Apple sponge cake

Light fluffy sponge with gorgeous soft apples, truly fabulous as a slice of cake with a cuppa but also warm with custard.

Ingredients
250g/9 oz butter, softened

250g/9 oz caster sugar

4 eggs

250g/9 oz self-raising flour

1 teaspoon vanilla extract

3 small apples, peeled, cored and sliced

2 tablespoons demerara sugar

1 teaspoon mixed spice

Method
Preheat your oven o 350F/180C/Gas 4.

Grease and line a 20cm cake tin.

Beat the sugar and butter together until light and fluffy. Add the eggs, flour and vanilla. Whisk to a smooth batter.

Pour into the prepared tin.

Lay the apple slices on top of the mix. They will look crowded, but don't worry, they shrink as they cook.

Mix the demerara sugar and the mixed spice together and sprinkle over the top of the apples.

Bake for just over an hour, until the sponge is risen and golden.

Options
Use sliced pears, plums or peaches instead of the apples.

Replace the mixed spice with ground cinnamon.

Banana choc chip muffins (vegan)

If you need to use up some very ripe bananas, this is the perfect recipe to do that.

Ingredients
250g/9 oz plain flour (all-purpose flour)
2 teaspoons baking powder
½ teaspoon bicarbonate soda
¼ teaspoon salt
50g/1 ¾ oz coconut oil (melted)
1 teaspoon vanilla extract
80g/2 ¾ oz sugar
4 small or 3 large bananas, mashed (the riper, the better)
40g/1 ½ oz chocolate chips

Method
Preheat the oven to 350F/180C/Gas 4.

Line a cupcake tray with paper cases, you should get 10-12 from this recipe.

Mix the flour, baking powder, bicarbonate soda and salt together. In a separate bowl mix the oil, sugar, mashed bananas and vanilla. Pour the wet ingredients into the dry and mix until combined. Stir the chocolate chips through.

Spoon into the cases, about two thirds full. Bake for about 20 minutes.

Fat apple rascals (vegan option)

With a name like that I had to make these, and they are delicious.

Traditionally just 'fat rascals' which date back to Elizabethan times they are also called Yorkshire tea biscuits. This recipe adds in apple to make them extra wonderful.

Ingredients
225g/8 oz self-raising flour
¼ teaspoon salt
110g/4 oz butter, cold and diced (vegan option)
75g/2 ½ oz soft light brown sugar
100g/3 ½ oz cooking apple, diced
50g/1 ¾ oz sultanas
3 tablespoons milk (any kind)
2 tablespoons demerara sugar
½ teaspoon ground cinnamon

Method
Pop the flour and salt into a bowl and rub in the butter until it resembles breadcrumbs.

Add in the soft light brown sugar, apples, sultanas and milk and bring together to form a dough.

Using two sheets of greased paper or cling wrap place the dough between and squash it into a flat disc. Wrap and chill for half an hour.

Preheat the oven to 350F/180C/Gas 4 and line two baking trays with baking parchment.

Flour a work surface and roll out the chilled dough as thinly as the chopped apples will allow. Cut into squares using a sharp knife and life them carefully onto the prepared trays, spacing them slightly apart.

Mix the demerara sugar and cinnamon together and sprinkle

over the squares.

Bake for about 20 minutes, until golden.

Options

Replace the apples with pears or dried apricots.

Apple crumble cake

Crumble is one of my favourite desserts, this recipe makes it into a cake - double whammy!

Ingredients
110g/4 oz butter
150g/5 ¼ oz soft light brown sugar
2 large eggs
210g/7.4 oz plain (all purpose) flour
1 teaspoon baking powder
Pinch of salt
1 teaspoon ground cinnamon
300g/10 ½ oz peeled, cored and sliced apple

Crumble topping:
50g/1 ¾ oz sugar
50g/1 ¾ oz plain (all purpose) flour
50g/1 ¾ oz butter

Method
Preheat the oven to 180C/350F/Gas 4. Grease and line a 20cm (8 inch) cake tin with a removable base.

Beat the butter and sugar until pale. Add the eggs one at a time mixing until they are incorporated.

Fold through the flour, baking powder, salt and cinnamon until you have a thick batter. Stir through the apple and pour into the cake tin. The batter will be thick so use a spatula or knife to even the top.

Blitz the crumble ingredients in a food processor (or blend with your fingertips by hand) until they resemble rough crumbs. Sprinkle the crumble topping over the batter.

Bake in the oven for 40-45 minutes or until baked through.

Options

Use peaches, apricots, pears or plums instead of apples.

Butter sugar cookies

Easy to make and soooooo delicious.

Ingredients
250g/9 oz plain flour (all purpose)
75g/2 ½ oz granulated sugar, plus more for the top
200g/7 oz butter, chopped
2 tablespoons finely grated unwaxed lemon zest
1 egg, lightly beaten

Method

Pop the flour into a bowl and mix in the sugar, butter and lemon zest, first by rubbing with your fingers and then by mixing with a spoon, until the dough is smooth and firm. Wrap in cling film and place in the refrigerator for one hour.

Preheat the oven to 190°C/375F/Gas 5.

Now place the dough between two sheets of baking parchment and roll it out to a rectangle about 1.5cm thick. Remove the top layer of baking parchment.

Brush the dough with egg and sprinkle sugar on top, don't be shy with the sugar, really heap it on. Carefully roll over it with a rolling pin, so the sugar is pressed slightly into the dough. Cut into 3 x 2cm pieces, place them on baking trays lined with fresh sheets of baking parchment and bake for 15-18 minutes.

Kicking hot chocolate

Hot chocolate with a fiery kick.

Ingredients
500ml/1-pint milk
4 squares dark chocolate
¼ teaspoon cinnamon
Pinch of cayenne pepper
Crushed chilli seeds (optional)

Method
Pop all the ingredients into a saucepan over a low heat and stir until just before it boils, and the chocolate has melted.

Serve topped with whipped cream and if you are feeling brave you can sprinkle it with crushed chilli seeds.

October

Corn and squash soup
Meatloaf
Patatas bravas
Coriander chutney
Coriander chutney chicken
Buckwheat and corn tortillas
Peanut bread
Gingerbread pudding cake
Parsnip and maple syrup cake
Irish barmbrack fruit loaf
Chocolate coconut cake bars
Souling cakes
Peanut butter choc chip cookies
Spiced chocolate butternut squash pie
Chai hot chocolate

October has quite possibly become the most celebrated pagan holiday, in the form of Samhain (Halloween). I love this time of the year; autumn is my favourite with the crisp fresh air first thing in the morning and the colour of the autumn trees. It is the end of summer and the third and final harvest of the year, a time when the veil between the worlds is at its thinnest, and a time to celebrate the lives of those that have passed and to remember and honour our ancestors. Oh … and eat lots of sweets.

Aside from all the Samhain goodies that will give us all a sugar overdose, foods for this season make me think of big hearty casseroles, home baked bread and stick to your rib puddings.

This is a basic list of produce that is usually in season during the month of October. It will obviously vary depending on where you are in the world and what the weather has been like. Be guided by what you find in your local greengrocers or farmers market. If you shop in the supermarket, check for labels that say it is 'new season'.

Aubergine/eggplant, beetroot, broccoli, Brussels sprouts, cabbage (green/white/red), carrots, cauliflower, celeriac, celery, chives, courgette/zucchinis, cucumber, fennel, French beans, garlic, leeks, mushrooms, onions, parsnips, peas, peppers & chillies, potatoes, pumpkins & squashes, radish, runner beans, spinach, swede, sweetcorn, tomatoes.

Apples, blackberries, damsons, grapes, melons, peaches & nectarines, pears, raspberries, outdoor rhubarb (UK).

Apples, cranberries, grapes, pomegranates (USA).

Corn and squash soup

This soup just says "hey, autumn come on in!".

Ingredients
1 butternut squash (or similar), peeled and diced
2 tablespoon olive or vegetable oil
1 large onion, chopped
1 jalapeno chilli, chopped (or ½ teaspoon dried chilli flakes)
2 cloves garlic, crushed
1 heaped teaspoon cumin seeds
1 tablespoon dried oregano
Salt and pepper
Large tin of sweetcorn or the kernels from 2 corn cobs
Tablespoon coriander (cilantro)
2 large tomatoes, chopped
1 litre/35 fl oz vegetable stock

Method
Heat the oil in a pan and add the onions, squash, chilli, garlic, cumin and oregano. Cook for about ten minutes on a low heat. Add the stock, tomatoes, corn, coriander and season with salt and pepper. Bring to the boil and then turn down the heat to simmer for twenty minutes until the squash is tender.

Options
Use pumpkin instead of squash.
This also works with sweet potatoes instead of squash.
If you like it hotter, double the chilli.
If you don't like coriander replace it with parsley.
The fresh tomatoes can be replaced with a tin of tomatoes, drained.

Meatloaf

This is a recipe that just screams home cooking comfort food. Serve it with plenty of mashed potato. Any left overs can be sliced and used in sandwiches. And it could not be simpler to make.

Ingredients
500g/1 lb beef mince
500g/1 lb pork & herb sausages (remove the skins)
1 onion, chopped
1 fat clove garlic, crushed
60g/2 oz porridge oats
Salt & pepper
1 egg

Method
Preheat the oven to 375F/Gas mark 5/190C.

Mix all the ingredients together in a bowl, the best way to do this is with your hands - it is squelchy but definitely the only way to incorporate everything properly and to break down the meat.

Mould your mixture into a flat loaf shape and pop in a roasting pan/dish.

Bake in the oven for about an hour.

Options
Brush the top of the meatloaf with tomato ketchup before you bake it.

Add in a handful of chopped chorizo.

Add in a few chopped bacon rashers.

Patatas bravas

A glorious Spanish spicy potato and tomato dish that is really simple to make.

Ingredients
8 potatoes
Olive or vegetable oil
2 onions, sliced
3 garlic cloves, crushed
1 teaspoon dried chilli flakes or 1 red chilli, sliced
1 large carrot, peeled and diced
1 teaspoon dried thyme
2 tins chopped tomatoes (400g x 2)
2 tablespoons cider vinegar
1 teaspoon dried rosemary
1 teaspoon paprika
Salt and pepper

Method
Dice the potatoes (I keep the skins on but peel if you prefer). Boil in salted water until tender (about 10 minutes). Drain.

Heat a tablespoon of oil in a pan and sauté the onion, garlic and chilli/chilli flakes for a couple of minutes. Add the diced carrot, paprika and the thyme and rosemary. Cook for another ten minutes on a gentle heat.

Add the chopped tomatoes and vinegar, season with salt and pepper. Simmer for ten minutes.

In a separate pan heat four tablespoons of oil and add the potatoes, fry for about ten minutes until they are golden and crispy.

Dish out the potatoes and cover them with the tomato sauce.

Options
If you like it really spicy, double the chilli and paprika.

Coriander (cilantro) chutney

Eat as a dip for chips, crisps or flat breads but it is also an ingredient in the coriander chicken recipe below.

Ingredients
100g/3 ½ oz coriander/cilantro (a large bunch)
60g/2 oz plain peanuts (unsalted and unroasted)
4 tablespoons of lemon juice
2 small green chillies, deseeded and finely chopped
1 teaspoon salt
¼ teaspoon turmeric
4 teaspoons brown sugar

Method
Wash and chop the coriander, add the peanuts and lemon juice, chillies, salt, turmeric and sugar. Pop the mix into a blender until it's got a pesto-like consistency.
It will keep for up to a week in a jar in the fridge.

Coriander (cilantro) chutney chicken

This is just delicious and well worth the effort of making your own coriander chutney.

Ingredients
5cm root ginger, peeled and chopped
6 cloves garlic, chopped
¾ green chilli, chopped
Salt
2 tablespoons vegetable oil
2 onions, finely sliced
4 chicken breasts or 8 boneless chicken thighs, chopped into bite size pieces
6 tablespoons coriander/cilantro chutney (recipe above)

Method
Crush the ginger, garlic and chilli in a pestle and mortar along with a pinch of salt to create a paste.

Put the oil in a large pan on a medium heat. Add the onions and fry for about five minutes then add in the ginger, garlic and chilli paste and cook for two minutes. Pop the chicken pieces into the pan and seal them on all sides.

Add in the coriander chutney, stir and put a lid on the pan. Turn the heat down to low and simmer for fifteen minutes until the chicken is cooked.

Options
Replace the chicken with tofu or diced butternut squash.

Buckwheat and corn tortillas

Seriously easy to make...

Ingredients
800ml/28 fl oz water
2 eggs
200g/7 oz cornmeal
259g/9 oz buckwheat flour
3 teaspoons salt

Method
Combine all the ingredients in large bowl & whisk well - add more water as needed 1/8 cup at a time (batter should be thin-more like cake batter than muffin batter.)

Heat a large non-stick frying pan or skillet over med-low heat.

Ladle in one scoop of batter like you would pancakes.

Take the backside of a spoon & smooth out the batter to the outer sides to get the tortilla as thin as you can & also even out the shape (this should make it more uniform in size & shape & help increase the size).

Allow to cook until browned - flip & brown the other side - be patient & watch closely.

Peanut bread

This bread is scrummy (if you like peanuts) and can be eaten as a sweet or savoury bread. Spread with just butter, jam or honey or cover in cream cheese. It is also delicious toasted.

Ingredients
500g/1 lb strong white flour
1 ½ teaspoon salt
7g/2 teaspoons quick action dry yeast
350ml/12 fl oz warm water
300g/10 ½ oz crunchy peanut butter

Method
Put the flour, salt, peanut butter and yeast into a bowl, slowly add the warm water mixing until you have a dough. Leave in the bowl to rest for two hours.

Grease a baking tray. Knock the air out of the dough and mould into two sausage shapes, approximately 50cm/20 inches long. Roll them up into a coil, place them on a baking tray and leave to prove for one hour.

Preheat the oven to 400F/200C/Gas 6.

Dust each loaf lightly with flour and bake for 25 minutes.

Gingerbread pudding cake

It is a cake...no, it's a pudding...whatever it is, I know it is lush!
Serve warm with custard, cream or ice cream.
Any leftovers are also nice eaten cold.

Ingredients
60g/2 oz butter
125g/4 ¼ oz golden syrup
100g/3 ½ oz plain flour (all purpose)
25g/0.8 oz self-raising flour
1 teaspoon bicarbonate of soda
1 heaped teaspoon ground ginger
Half a teaspoon mixed spice
100g/3 ½ oz caster sugar
Pinch of salt
125ml/4.3 fl oz milk
1 egg, beaten

Method

Grease and line a 20cm square cake tin or a 2lb loaf tin. Pre-heat oven to 170c/gas mark 3.

Put butter and golden syrup in a saucepan and melt over a low heat, stirring occasionally, then remove from heat.

Sift both flours, the soda and the spices into a mixing bowl. Add the sugar and salt, give it a good stir, then add the egg and milk mixing until smooth. Gradually add the melted butter/ syrup mix, stirring until well combined.

Pour the batter into the prepared tin and bake for 50-55mins until risen and firm to the touch. Allow to cool in the tin for 5mins before turning out onto a wire rack.

Parsnip and maple syrup cake

Parsnips in a cake? What is this madness? Truly scrumptious, that's what it is!

Ingredients
175g/6 oz butter
250g/9 oz demerara sugar
100ml/3 ½ fl oz maple syrup
3 large eggs
250g/9 oz self-raising flour
2 teaspoons baking powder
2 teaspoons mixed spice
250g/9 oz parsnips, peeled and grated
1 medium eating apple, peeled, cored and grated

Method

Preheat your oven to 350F/180C/gas 4.

Grease 2 x 20cm sandwich tins and line the bases with baking parchment.

Melt butter, sugar and maple syrup in a pan over gentle heat, then cool slightly.

Whisk the eggs into this mixture, then stir in the flour, baking powder and mixed spice, followed by the grated parsnip and apple.

Divide between the tins, then bake for 25-30 mins until the tops spring back when pressed lightly.

Cool the cakes slightly in the tins before turning out onto wire racks to cool completely.

I like to fill this cake with a jar of caramel spread, but you could use buttercream or a cream cheese filling. I just top it with an icing sugar and water mix then crumbled over some fudge.

Irish barmbrack fruit loaf

A really traditional sweet cake loaf packed full of all sorts of gorgeous dried fruits and flavoured with tea.

Ingredients
300g/10 ½ oz mixed dried fruit (sultanas, currants, raisins, candied peel)
200g/7 oz light brown sugar
250g/9 oz self-raising flour
1 cup cold strong black tea
1 egg
1 teaspoon mixed spice (cinnamon, clove, nutmeg)

Method
Soak the mixed fruit in the cold tea for about 6 hours, overnight if you can.
Pre heat the oven to 180C/350F/Gas 4 and line a 1lb loaf tin with greased baking paper.
Mix together all the ingredients and pour into the loaf pan. Bake for 1-1 ½ hours or until cooked through.
Serve buttered.

Options
Ring the changes by using different types of tea such as Earl Grey or spiced chai.

Chocolate coconut cake bars

These are totally lush...if you like a certain branded coconut chocolate confection then you will love these, only this one is much better...For the best result keep them in the fridge.

Ingredients
Tin of coconut milk (not the lite version, we need the full fat for this)
100g/3 ½ oz desiccated coconut
20g/ ¾ oz coconut flakes, crushed
5 tablespoons golden syrup
200g/7 oz dark chocolate (dairy free if you are vegan)
30g/1 oz mixed seeds or crushed nuts (optional)

Method
We don't need the whole tin of coconut milk, just the coconut cream that sets at the top - not the coconut water. Scoop out 150g (5 ¼ oz) of the coconut cream. Use the coconut water to drink!

Mix the coconut cream with the golden syrup, desiccated coconut, flaked coconut and seeds or nuts if you are using until it is all combined.

Take scoopfuls of the mixture and shape it into 10 balls, mounds or bar shapes, whatever takes your fancy. Pop them on a tray and put it in the freezer for about an hour to set.

Break the chocolate into pieces and pop in a microwave bowl and melt. Or put the chocolate in a heat proof bowl over a pan of hot water. Stir until melted.

Take the coconut shapes from the freezer and cover with the melted chocolate. This is a bit fiddly, either pop the shapes onto a wire rack and spoon over the chocolate or dip the coconut shapes into the melted chocolate and roll it around until covered. Either way it can get messy!

Sprinkle a few seeds or crushed nuts on the top if you want to.

Souling cakes

These are called 'cakes' but are actually cookies. Traditionally baked on All Souls' Day when children visited villages begging for food. Going back in history even further these were believed to have been left on graves for the dead.

Ingredients
350g/12 ¼ oz plain flour (all purpose)
175g/6 oz caster sugar
175g/6 oz butter, softened
1 egg
½ teaspoon ground cinnamon
½ teaspoon mixed spice
Pinch nutmeg
1 ½ teaspoons cider vinegar

Method
Preheat your oven to 350F/180C/Gas 4. Grease two baking sheets.
Mix all the dry ingredients together and rub in the butter. Add the egg and vinegar and mix together to form a soft dough.
On a floured surface, roll out to about 5mm/ ¼" and cut into rounds with a cookie cutter. Place on the prepared trays.
Bake for 15-20 minutes until lightly golden.

Peanut butter choc chip cookies

This recipe makes quite a big batch of cookies, perfect for parties or rituals.

Ingredients
225g/8 oz butter or margarine
200g/7 oz brown sugar
200g/7 oz granulated sugar
2 eggs
250g/9 oz peanut butter
2 teaspoons baking soda
½ teaspoon salt
360g/12 ½ oz plain (all purpose) flour
90g/3 oz chocolate chip cookies (optional)

Method
Preheat the oven to 180C/350F/Gas 4.
Cream the butter and both sugars together.
Add eggs and beat.
Stir in peanut butter, baking soda and salt. (and choc chips if using)
Gradually mix in the flour.
Form dough into 1" balls and place on ungreased cookie sheets (I just spooned dollops onto the baking trays!)
Squash with a fork dipped in flour into 2" circles.
Bake for 8-10 minutes or until cookies are a pale, golden colour.

Spiced chocolate butternut squash pie

Yep, I know this is dessert and I know it includes a vegetable but trust me it works. Add in the chocolate and top with sweet meringue or whipped cream and you can't go wrong.

Ingredients
1 medium butternut squash or 2 small butternut squash
300g/10 ½ oz can evaporated milk
100g/3 ½ oz sugar
2 eggs
1 teaspoon ground cinnamon
½ teaspoon ground ginger
150g/5 ¼ oz dark chocolate
9-inch deep dish pastry pie crust

For the Italian meringue:
180g/6 ¼ oz caster sugar
3 large egg whites
1 tablespoon lemon juice
60ml/2 fl oz water

Method
Pierce the squash with a knife in several places, and place in a baking dish in the oven at 180C/350F/Gas 4. Bake until the squash is tender and easily pierced with a knife (about 1 hour) then allow to cool completely. Cut the squash in half and remove the seeds.

Scoop out about the pulp and place in your blender or food processor. Add all remaining ingredients except the chocolate and blend until smooth.

Melt the chocolate in the microwave or over a pan of water and then pour into your squash mixture, stir until combined. Pour into a prepared pastry pie crust.

Bake for 45-50 minutes or until the centre is nearly set, and the pie is starting to slightly pull away from the edges of the pan. Cool on a wire rack.

You can eat the pie as it is or add big dollops of whipped cream on top.

I topped mine with Italian meringue which doesn't require baking. It can be a bit tricky but isn't really as scary as it sounds although you do need a confectionery thermometer.

Put all but 3 tablespoons of the sugar and the water into a small saucepan with a confectionery thermometer. Set over a medium high heat and allow to heat up.

The temperature will rise quite quickly until the sugar reaches 100°C when the water boils, then more slowly until the sugar reaches 121°C. (This may be indicated as 'soft ball' on your thermometer.)

Meanwhile, whisk the egg whites and remaining sugar in the bowl of a stand mixer fitted with the whisk attachment. Once they begin to form soft peaks, add the lemon juice.

Once the egg whites have formed stiff peaks and the sugar has reached 121°C, it's time to combine them. Turn the mixer on to full power and pour a steady stream of the molten sugar into the bowl. Make sure you don't hit the whisk with the sugar, as this will shoot the sugar all around the sides of the bowl, welding it there so it doesn't cook the egg whites. Once all the molten sugar has been added, the bowl should be pretty hot. Leave the mixer on full speed until the bowl has cooled fully; this should take around 10 minutes. Once cooled down, you can spoon or pipe the meringue on top of the pie (it is now totally safe to eat as you have cooked the eggs).

Chai hot chocolate

Mmmm....my personal favourite. This spicy version of hot chocolate could not be easier.

Ingredients
250ml/9 fl oz milk (any kind)
Two squares of either dark, milk or plain chocolate
A teaspoon or two of sugar
1 teaspoon ground cinnamon
Pinch of ground nutmeg
Pinch of ground cardamom

Method
Pop all the ingredients into a saucepan. Heat gently until the milk is warm. Whisk together and et voila - your chai hot chocolate is ready.

November

French onion soup
Bacon roly poly
Potato quesadillas
Fried chicken
Chappatis
Sweet rolls
Treacle tart
Spiced carrot traybake
Chocolate traybake
Chocolate puddle pudding
Chocolate brownie flapjacks
Viennese biscuits
Greek halva pudding
Squirrel hot chocolate

Leading on from the last harvest, November still has a huge abundance of gorgeous produce to work with, but we are winding down now. Preparations are being made for the winter.

The weather will also be colder now, the warm summer months seeming so distant. Lots of lovely big hearty meals are the way to go.

This is a basic list of produce that is usually in season during the month of November. It will obviously vary depending on where you are in the world and what the weather has been like. Be guided by what you find in your local greengrocers or farmers market. If you shop in the supermarket, check for labels that say it is 'new season'.

Beetroot, broccoli, Brussels sprouts, cabbages (green/white/red), carrots, cauliflower, celeriac, celery, chives, greens, lettuce, leeks, mushrooms, onions, parsnips, peppers & chillies, potatoes, pumpkins & squashes, radish, spinach, swede, sweetcorn, tomatoes.

Apples, pears, raspberries (UK).

Oranges, pears, pomegranates, tangerines (USA).

French onion soup

This is what I make when I have tons of onions, we ate it in Montmartre a few years ago - but named it 'cheese soup' because the French do like to put huge amounts of cheese sliced baguette on top - and I am not going to argue with that.

Ingredients
50g/1 ¾ oz butter
3 large onions, sliced
10ml/2 teaspoons plain (all purpose) flour
1 litre/35 fl oz vegetable (or chicken) stock
60ml/4 tablespoons white wine OR 30ml/2 tablespoons dry sherry
4/6 slices crusty bread
150g/5 ¼ oz Gruyere or Emmenthal cheese
Salt & pepper

Method
Slice the onions and pop them in a big saucepan with the butter - don't be tempted to use margarine it really doesn't work as well.

Cook the onions over a low heat for about 10 to 15 minutes, stirring occasionally, until they are lightly browned. Don't rush this stage!

Stir in the flour and continue to cook, stirring continuously until the flours turns a light sandy colour.

Pour in the stock and the alcohol.

Bring to the boil, stirring continuously.

Season with salt and pepper, cover and simmer for 15 minutes.

To serve I find it easiest to scoop out the onions with a slotted spoon into serving bowls then top up with the liquid.

Toast the slices of bread under the grill then sprinkle the cheese on top. Return to the grill and melt the cheese. Place the cheesy toasts onto of the soup once it is served into bowls.

Options

I often make this without the alcohol, and it works very well but you might want to substitute by putting in a few dashes of Worcestershire sauce instead or a tablespoon of yeast extract. You can substitute the butter for oil, but you need to cook it really slowly so that the onions caramelise.

Bacon roly poly

This is an old recipe, one my grandmother used to make when we were children and I love it. This one is baked rather than steamed, it is quicker, and I like the texture the baking gives to the outside.

Ingredients
170g/6 oz self-raising flour
85g/3 oz shredded suet (I prefer to use vegetable suet, but you can use beef)
Salt and pepper
A little water
Milk or egg for glazing
200g/7 oz bacon rashers, chopped
1 onion, finely chopped
2 teaspoons dried parsley

Method
Preheat the oven to 200C/400F/Gas 6.

Fry the bacon and onions gently until just cooked.

In a large bowl mix together the flour, suet, parsley and salt and pepper. Add a little bit of cold water at a time and combine to form a soft dough.

Roll out the dough on a floured surface. You want it to be a rectangle about 12 x 9 inches.

Spread the bacon and onion mixture over the surface of the dough leaving a gap around the edges.

Dampen the edges and then roll it up. Seal the ends and pop onto a baking tray lined with parchment paper. Brush with egg milk.

Bake in the oven for half an hour, until golden.

Potato quesadillas

I had some leftover baked potatoes so looking for inspiration I found the idea of mashed potato quesadillas...

Ingredients
8 flour tortillas
650g/23 oz mashed potato or 4/6 baked potatoes
1 onion, sliced
1 red bell pepper, sliced
1 fat clove of garlic, crushed
½ teaspoon cumin seeds
Salt & pepper
½ teaspoon dried basil
½ teaspoon dried oregano
Olive oil
125g/4 ½ oz grated cheese (cheddar or vegan)

Method
Sauté the sliced onions, peppers and garlic in some olive oil for a few minutes adding in the cumin seeds and dried herbs.

If you are using baked potatoes mash them with the skins on (I popped them in the food processor).

Add the potato and salt and pepper to the pan giving it a good stir, sauté on a low heat for a few minutes, remove from the heat and stir the grated cheese through.

Take one of the flour tortillas and spread some of the potato mix over it then add another tortilla on top and press down.

Carefully pop the filled tortilla into a dry non-stick frying pan on a low heat and cook for about a minute, then very carefully flip it over and cook for a minute on the other side until nicely golden.

Remove from the pan slice into four and serve.

Options

The options for these are endless! Basically, you need the cheese to make the tortillas stick together, other than that the world is your lobster, stick whatever you want inside them.

Chopped chicken or ham works well.

Make it seriously cheesy by adding mozzarella.

Add sliced guacamole and chopped fresh tomato.

Fried chicken

This is a huge favourite with our children.

Ingredients
236ml/8.3 fl oz milk or buttermilk
1 teaspoon mustard powder
1 teaspoon salt
4 large chicken breasts
280g/10 oz self-raising flour
1 tablespoon freshly ground black pepper
1 teaspoon powdered garlic
1 teaspoon turmeric
1 teaspoon dried thyme
1 teaspoon dried oregano/marjoram
½ teaspoon cayenne
Oil for deep frying.

Method
Pour the milk into a large dish and stir in the mustard powder and salt.

Slice the chicken breasts into two or three pieces each breast depending on how large they are then place them in the milk. Leave them to sit for about 20 minutes to half an hour.

In a separate bowl mix together the flour and all the other dry ingredients.

Heat the oil in a large pan or deep fat fryer.

Remove each piece of chicken from the milk and drop it into the flour mixture turning to coat evenly.

Using tongs place each piece of chicken into the fat, cook on each side for about 3-4 minutes until golden brown and crispy. Remove and drain on paper towels. You will need to cook the chicken in batches so keep the first lot warm in a low oven until ready to serve.

Chappatis

These are lovely to have with a curry or soup.

Ingredients
Makes 8

1 mug of wholemeal chapatti flour, or half regular wholemeal and half plain white flour, plus extra for dusting the dough

½ teaspoon salt

3 tablespoon vegetable oil, plus 1 teaspoon extra

½-¾ mug of water

Method
Put the flour into a bowl, add the salt and mix together. Make a well in the middle add 3 tbsp of oil and mix, using your fingers, until it resembles fine breadcrumbs. Pour in ½ mug of water, then add the rest little by little - you may not need all of it - until you can knead the mixture into a soft and pliable dough; this will take around 6-8 minutes.

Divide your dough into 8 pieces. Put the frying pan on a medium to high heat. Take one piece of dough, roll it into a ball between your palms, coat it generously with flour, flatten it into a disc and then roll it out to around 10cm in diameter. Lightly coat both sides in flour, roll it out to around 16cm and put it face side down on the hot pan.

Wait for the edges to colour white and for the chapatti to start to bubble (30-40 seconds), then turn it over and cook the chapatti for the same amount of time. Turn it over again - it should start to puff up at this point, so press it down gently with the flat side of the spatula - for around 10 seconds, then turn it over again and do the same. Check that all the dough is cooked (any uncooked spots will look dark and doughy) and put on to a plate. Cover with a towel or wrap in foil to keep warm, then repeat.

Sweet rolls

They are slightly sweet and very soft.

Ingredients
4 ½ teaspoons dry yeast (2 packets)
500ml/1-pint warm milk
180g/6 ¼ oz honey
6 tablespoons butter, melted plus a little more for greasing
2 large eggs, room temperature
1 tablespoon salt
1275g/45 oz plain flour (all purpose)

Method
Add the yeast and honey to the milk and stir. Leave to stand for about five minutes.

Add the butter, eggs, salt and half the flour, mixing until smooth.

Add the remaining flour gradually until it comes together as a dough. Kneed for ten minutes. Pop into a greased bowl, cover and allow to rise until double the size, about an hour.

Grease two baking sheets.

Knock back the dough and roll out to a rectangle about 1" (2cm) deep. Cut into 48 rolls (6 rows, each one cut into 8 rolls).

Place the rolls on the baking sheets spaced a little apart.

Cover and allow to prove until double in size, about an hour.

Preheat the oven to 350F/180C/Gas 4.

Bake in the oven for 12-15 minutes until golden brown.

Treacle tart

I have often found treacle tart to be dry and disappointing when I have eaten it in the past, but this recipe is a game changer. Gorgeously soft and gooey.

Ingredients
220g/7 ¾ oz fresh white breadcrumbs
600g/21 oz golden syrup

For the pastry:
180g/6 ¼ oz plain flour (all purpose)
90g/3 oz butter
2 to 3 tablespoons water

Method
Preheat your oven to 400F/200C/Gas 6. Lightly grease a tart tin.

Rub the butter into the flour until it resembles breadcrumbs, pour in the cold water a small amount at a time and bring together to form a dough. Roll out on a lightly floured surface and fit into a tart tin. Prick the base of the pastry with a fork. Pop the tart case into the fridge for half an hour to rest.

Then pop a piece of baking parchment into the tart case and fill with dried/baking beans. Bake in the oven for ten minutes. Remove the paper and beans and return the pastry case to the oven for a further ten minutes.

Mix the breadcrumbs with the golden syrup and pour this mixture into the baked pastry case.

Turn the oven down to 350F/180C/Gas 4.

Bake the filled tart for half an hour.

Leave to rest for ten minutes then serve.

Spiced carrot traybake

Easy peasy and very scrummy.

Ingredients
275g/9 ¾ oz self-raising flour
350g/12 ¼ oz caster sugar
2 teaspoons baking powder
3 teaspoons ground cinnamon
2 teaspoons ground ginger
300ml/10 ½ fl oz vegetable oil
275g/9 ¾ oz grated carrots
4 large eggs
1 teaspoon vanilla extract

Icing:
8 tablespoons icing sugar (powdered sugar)
Cold water to mix

Method
Preheat your oven to 350F/180C/gas mark 4.

Grease a 12 x 9" traybake tin and line it with baking parchment.

Add all of the dry cake ingredients to a bowl; then add the oil, grated carrots, eggs (one at a time) and the vanilla extract, beating between each addition. Pour into your prepared tray and level the surface. Bake in the oven for 50-60 minutes or until the cake is well risen, golden brown and a skewer comes out clean. Allow to cool in the tin for 10 minutes (or leave to cool in the tin completely) then turn out onto a wire rack.

To make the icing slowly add cold water to the icing sugar a teaspoon at a time and mix until you have a thick dropping consistency, then 'drizzle' the icing over the cake.

This cuts into 12 seriously big squares or 20 smaller ones (but who wants a small piece of cake?).

Chocolate traybake

This is so easy and quick to make but tastes delicious. I usually don't bother to ice it, but you could top it with butter cream or melted chocolate if you wanted to.

Ingredients
4 level tablespoons cocoa powder
4 tablespoons hot water
225g/8 oz butter, softened
225g/8 oz sugar
275g/9 ¾ oz self-raising flour
2 level teaspoons baking powder
4 large eggs
4 tablespoons milk
30 x 23cm (12 x 9 inch) baking tin

Method
Preheat the oven to 180C/350F/gas 4. Grease and line the base of a baking tin.

Blend the cocoa powder with the hot water and allow to cool slightly.

Pop all the ingredients into a bowl and mix until well blended. Spoon into the prepared tin and level the surface.

Bake for 35-40 minutes or until the cake has shrunk from the sides and springs back when pressed lightly in the centre with your fingertips.

Leave to cool in the tin.

Options
Pop a handful of chocolate chips into the mixture.

Add a teaspoon of ground cinnamon or ginger to spice it up.

Chocolate puddle pudding (vegan option)

When I left home at the tender age of 17 and moved in with a pig farmer (long story...) this was one of the recipes I made a lot in my new home... I had forgotten about it until recently, it is seriously easy to make.

Ingredients
175g/6 oz self-raising flour
150g/5 ¼ oz soft brown sugar
50g/1 ¾ oz cocoa powder
150ml/5 fl oz milk (any kind)
2 teaspoons vanilla essence
50g/1 ¾ oz butter, melted (or vegan margarine)
50g/1 ¾ oz soft brown sugar
500ml/1-pint hot water

Method
Mix the flour and sugar with half the cocoa. Beat in the milk, essence and melted butter and then pour into a buttered 1.4 litre (2 ½ pint) ovenproof dish. Mix the remaining cocoa with the smaller amount of sugar and sprinkle over the top.

Pour the water over the pudding and bake at Gas 4/180C/350F for about 1 hour.

The sponge should be crusty and cooked with a lush sauce underneath.

Serve hot.

Chocolate brownie flapjacks

If a mummy brownie and a daddy flapjack love each other very much... this is their offspring and it is wickedly good. Why choose between a brownie or a flapjack when you can have both?

Ingredients

Flapjack layer:
150g/5 ¼ oz butter
150g/5 ¼ oz soft brown sugar
140g/5 oz golden syrup
325g/11 ½ oz porridge oats
100g/3 ½ oz mixed seeds

Brownie layer:
2 eggs
225g/8 oz caster sugar
140g/5 oz butter
60g/2 oz cocoa powder
60g/2 oz plain flour (all-purpose flour)
40g/1 ½ oz dark chocolate chips

Method

Preheat your oven to 300F/150C/Gas 2. Line a 20cm x 32cm baking tray with parchment.

Start by making the flapjacks. Melt the butter, sugar and golden syrup in a pan over a gentle heat. Add the porridge oats and seeds. Mix together.

Then for the brownie, whisk together the eggs and sugar until they are light and fluffy. Melt the butter and whisk in the cocoa powder. Add the butter mixture to the eggs and sugar, mix and then fold in the flour and chocolate chips.

Spread the flapjack mixture on the base of the lined baking tin.

Next pour the brownie mixture over the top.

Bake for 35-40 minutes, the brownie will be slightly cracked on the top.

Cut into squares.

Viennese biscuits (cookies)

These are delicious melt in the mouth biscuits (cookies). You could sandwich two together with buttercream and jam if you were feeling particularly energetic.

Ingredients
250g/9 oz butter, softened
100g/3 ½ oz icing sugar (powdered sugar), sifted
1 teaspoon vanilla extract
250g/9 oz plain (all purpose) flour
30g/1 oz cornflour
½ teaspoon baking powder
Pinch salt
1 tablespoon milk

Method
Line two baking sheets with baking parchment.

Pop the butter into a mixer and beat for 2-3 minutes until it is soft, light and pale - the butter needs to be really soft.

Add the icing sugar and vanilla and beat for a further 3 minutes until smooth and soft.

Sift the flour, cornflour, baking powder and salt into the bowl with the butter mixture and mix, add the milk and mix again to combine.

Spoon the dough into a piping bag fitted with a star nozzle and pipe 5cm rosette shaped spirals onto the baking sheets (you should get 20 biscuits from this mixture). Allow a little space for each one to spread slightly.

Chill the biscuits for 20 minutes in the fridge while you pre-heat the oven to 170C/325F/Gas 3.

Bake on the middle shelf in the oven for 10-12 minutes until the biscuits are pale golden at the edges.

Cool on the baking sheet for five minutes then carefully transfer them to a wire rack to cool completely.

Greek halva pudding (vegan)

This semolina dish doesn't look the prettiest, but it tastes lush. And it is also vegan.

Ingredients
118ml/4 fl oz olive oil
118ml/4 fl oz vegetable/corn oil
340g/12 oz semolina
90g/3 oz sultanas

For the syrup:
675g/24 oz of sugar
1 litre/35 fl oz water
1 teaspoon ground cinnamon

Method
Start by preparing the syrup. Add the syrup ingredients into a pan over a high heat and bring to the boil. Boil until the sugar has dissolved and the syrup slightly thickens. Set aside but keep warm.

To prepare the halva heat the oil in a large pan and gradually mix in the semolina. Stir constantly to allow the semolina to absorb the oil. When the semolina starts to bubble turn the heat down and allow it to toast until golden (keep stirring). Be careful not to over toast it otherwise it will taste bitter. Remove the pan from the heat and pour in the warm syrup. Stir and return the pan to the heat. Cook whilst stirring until the mixture thickens and pulls away easily from the sides of the pan.

Remove the pan from the heat and stir in the sultanas. Cover the halva with a tea towel and let it rest for ten minutes. Then pour the mixture into a serving dish. Allow to cool for a couple of hours and garnish with ground cinnamon.

Squirrel hot chocolate

OK it's not actually made from squirrels, but if they drank hot chocolate, I bet they would love this one.

Ingredients
500ml/1-pint milk
3 teaspoons Nutella spread (chocolate nut spread)

Method
Warm the milk in a saucepan then whisk in the Nutella…sorted.

December

Vegetable, bean and pasta soup
Dorset jugged steak
Vegetable and cheese crumble
Cheese and Marmite pasties
Sage and onion bread
Fougasse
Bread pudding
German butter cake
Spice muffins
Sprinkle cookies
Coconut truffles
Digestive biscuits
Spice bombs
Mulled wine hot chocolate

The winter solstice of Yule, as it is often called, arrives in December. The shortest day and the longest night, it is from this day onwards that we start to get a little bit more sunlight each day. A time for family, friends, get togethers, feasting and celebrating.

We probably all over eat at this time of the year, I like to think of it as fuel to help keep my body warm... The scents and tastes at Yule are amazing with cinnamon and cloves being my favourites, just the smell of mince pies baking in the oven sums up this season for me.

This is a basic list of produce that is usually in season during the month of December. It will obviously vary depending on where you are in the world and what the weather has been like. Be guided by what you find in your local greengrocers or farmers market. If you shop in the supermarket, check for labels that say it is 'new season'.

Beetroot, broccoli, Brussels sprouts, cabbages (green/white/ red), carrots, cauliflower, celeriac, celery, greens, leeks, lettuce, mushrooms, onions, parsnips, potatoes, pumpkins & squashes, radish, spinach, swede.

Apples, forced rhubarb, pears (UK).

Grapefruit, oranges, papayas, pears, pomegranates, tangerines (USA).

Vegetable, bean and pasta soup

This is a real warmer and fills you up really well.

Ingredients
3 tablespoons olive or vegetable oil
1 onion, chopped
4 cloves garlic, crushed
1 teaspoon dried oregano
1 teaspoon dried thyme
Half head of cauliflower, cut into florets
Half head of broccoli, cut into florets
2 carrots, peeled and diced
2 cans of beans, drained (butter, cannelloni, haricot or mixed)
(440g x 2)
2 litres/4 pints vegetable stock
Handful of pasta shapes or broken spaghetti
Salt and pepper

Method
Heat the oil in a pan and fry the onion on a low heat for about ten minutes. Add the garlic and cook for a further couple of minutes. Add the herbs, broccoli, cauliflower and carrots. Simmer for five minutes. Stir in the beans and add the stock. Bring to the boil then simmer for fifteen minutes. Add the pasta and cook for a further five to ten minutes, until it is all cooked. Season with salt and pepper.

Options
Use a whole head of broccoli and no cauliflower.
Use a whole head of cauliflower and no broccoli.
Substitute the carrots for sliced green/French beans.
Sprinkle with Parmesan cheese shavings to serve.

Dorset jugged steak

A traditional dish from Dorset in England, this was apparently eaten on the days when the fair came to town. Jugging is a term used for slow cooking. It is definitely a rich feasting dish.

Ingredients
700g/1 ½ lbs stewing steak, cubed
25g/0.8 oz plain (all purpose) flour
1 onion, sliced
4 cloves
Salt and pepper
150ml/ 5 fl oz port (or red wine if you don't have port)
450ml/ ¾ pint beef stock
225g/8 oz sausage meat
50g/1 ¾ oz breadcrumbs
2 tablespoons parsley
1 tablespoon redcurrant jelly

Method
Pre-heat the oven to 170C/325F/Gas 5.
Roll the meat cubes in the flour and pop them into a casserole dish. Add the onions and cloves and season. Pour in the port and the stock so that it covers the meat.
Put a lid on the casserole dish and put into the oven for three hours, until the meat is tender.
Mix the sausage meat, breadcrumbs and parsley together and season. Form the mixture into eight balls. Forty minutes before the end of the cooking time stir the redcurrant jelly into the casserole. Add the meat balls and cook without a lid for the remainder of the cooking time, until the sausage meat is cooked and slightly browned.

Vegetable and cheese crumble

I know this sounds like a relic from the 1970s, but it really does make a good homely comfort food.

Ingredients
1 onion, sliced

2 tablespoons vegetable oil

1 teaspoon dried rosemary

2 potatoes, diced

2 parsnips, peeled and diced

2 sweet potatoes, peeled and diced

1 courgette (zucchini), diced

250ml/9 fl oz vegetable stock

1 tablespoon plain (all purpose) flour

For the crumble:
100g/3 ½ oz bread

Salt and pepper

100g/3 ½ oz cheese, grated

Method
Sauté the onion in the oil in a large pan, cook it slowly for about five minutes. Add the rosemary and the vegetables. Pop a lid on the pan and simmer gently for about ten minutes.

Pour in the stock, plain flour and season with salt and pepper.

Pre heat the oven to 180C/350F/Gas 4.

To make the crumble whizz the bread in a blender or processor until it is crumbs. Season with salt and pepper and mix in the grated cheese.

Remove the lid from the casserole. Sprinkle the breadcrumb mix over the top of the vegetables.

Pop the casserole in the oven for half an hour, until the crumble is golden brown.

Options

Swap the rosemary for thyme or parsley.

Add in a handful of cooked bacon or chicken.

Swap the parsnips for carrots.

Swap the sweet potatoes for butternut squash.

Cheese and Marmite pasties (vegan option)

The pasty is a time-honoured tradition within Britain but every culture has its own variation of a filling wrapped in pastry. This one calls upon the savoury flavour of Marmite (or Vegemite) to give it a bit of a kick.

Ingredients
500g/1 lb potatoes, peeled and grated
200g/7 oz cheese, grated (Cheddar or a vegan/vegetarian alternative)
4 spring onions (scallions), sliced
100g/3 ½ oz fresh breadcrumbs
2 tablespoons Marmite (or Vegemite)

Pastry:
400g/14 oz plain flour (all-purpose flour)
275g/9 ¾ oz margarine, butter or vegan margarine
4 tablespoons water

Method
To make the pastry, rub the fat into the flour and then slowly add the water, until it comes together as a dough. Wrap it in cling film and pop into the fridge for 20 minutes.

Put the grated potato, cheese, breadcrumbs and spring onions into a bowl, season with salt and pepper and mix.

Preheat the oven to 170C/325F/Gas 3.

Roll out the pastry and using a saucer or bowl cut out six circles from the pastry. Warm the Marmite in a pan with a splash of water so that it becomes a little runnier. Brush the Marmite into the centre of each pastry circle, leaving a border around the edge.

Divide the filling between each circle of pastry. Wet the edges and fold the pastry over/up to cover the filing. Seal the edges and pinch/crimp. Pop the pasties onto a baking sheet. Brush the pasty with Marmite or milk and bake for 50 mins to 1 hour, until golden brown and crisp.

Sage and onion bread

This loaf has the lush flavours of fried onions and sage. It is delicious with soup but also served with cheese for lunch.

Ingredients
1 ½ teaspoons dried yeast
300ml/10 ½ fl oz warm milk (any kind)
1 large onion, finely diced
25g/0.8 oz butter or 1 tablespoon vegetable oil
200g/7 oz strong white bread flour
250g/9 oz strong wholemeal flour
1 teaspoon salt
Pepper
2 tablespoons fresh sage, chopped or 1 teaspoon dried sage

Method
Sprinkle the dried yeast onto the warm milk. Leave for 15 minutes until it is frothy.

Fry the onion in the butter or oil and cook for about five minutes until the onion is soft but not browned.

Mix the flours, salt, pepper and sage in a large bowl. Pop the onion and the yeast liquid into the flour. Mix until it forms a dough.

Knead for about 10 minutes (or 5 minutes in a mixer with a dough hook).

Tip back into the bowl, cover and leave to rise for about an hour, to double in size.

Turn the dough out onto a floured surface and dived into two. Shape into rounds and place on a greased baking tray.

Cover and leave in a warm place to rise again, for about half an hour.

Preheat the oven to 450F/230C/Gas 8. Bake on this high heat for about 15 minutes then reduce the temperature to 400F/200C/

Gas 6 and bake for a further 15 minutes.
It should be well risen and golden brown.

Fougasse

This is a fancy bread, a favourite that my youngest likes to make. It has a really lovely crust to it and is shaped like a leaf or an ear of wheat.

Ingredients
200ml/7 fl oz warm water
350g/12 ¼ oz strong white bread flour
1 teaspoon salt
7g/2 teaspoons (1 sachet) dried yeast
1 teaspoon dried thyme

Method
Put the flour in a bowl with the salt, stir in the yeast and the thyme.

Slowly add the warm water, stirring to bring the dough together.

Knead the dough for ten minutes.

Pop in an oiled bowl and cover, leave to prove until double in size, about an hour.

Cover a baking sheet with parchment paper.

Roll/pat the dough gently out to an oval shape about 20 x 25cm. Carefully lift it onto the baking sheet. Cover and leave to rise again for about an hour.

Preheat the oven to 450F/230C/Gas 8.

Using a sharp knife, cut 4 or 5 slits in the dough, so that it looks like the veins of a leaf.

Prise the slips open a little with your fingers to make them larger.

Spray the oven with water and bake the bread for 15 minutes, until it is a lovely golden brown.

Bread pudding

I love bread pudding but sometimes the stuff you find in shops is really dry, this however is a lovely recipe and my 'go to'. Eat as it is, but also good with custard or cream. I am pretty sure I have given myself a self-induced bread pudding coma eating so much of this stuff...

Ingredients
450g/15 ¾ oz bread (can be white or brown)

500ml/1-pint milk (any kind)

100g/3 ½ oz butter, melted

150g/5 ¼ oz soft brown sugar (use demerara or white if not available) + 2 tablespoons for topping

4 level teaspoons mixed spice

2 eggs, beaten

350g/12 oz dried mixed fruit (currants, raisins, sultanas, candied peel)

Two apples peeled and grated

Freshly grated nutmeg

Method
Preheat oven to 180C/350F/Gas 4.

Line an oblong baking tray with baking parchment. 12 x 9 x 2 inches (approx. 31 x 23 x 5 cm) but the exact size is not crucial as long as the container is big enough for the mixture.

Either tear the bread into small pieces or blitz to make breadcrumbs depending on how smooth you want the finished pudding, if the crust is particularly tough you might want to discard them and just use the bread inside. Pour over the milk, stir and leave for about 30 minutes so the bread is well soaked.

Add the melted butter, sugar, mixed spice and beaten eggs. Beat the mixture well until there are no lumps. Stir in the mixed fruit and grated apple.

Spoon into the baking tray and sprinkle with the two tablespoons of sugar and grated nutmeg.

Bake in the pre-heated oven for about 1¼-1½ hours.

Options

Replace the milk with orange juice.

You can also vary the dried fruit you add; dried apricot, dried pineapple and cherries also work well.

German butter cake

I kept seeing this being made on the food channel, so I had to investigate. This cake is seriously good.

Ingredients
600g/21 oz plain (all purpose) flour
Plus 70g/2 ½ oz plain flour if necessary
2 ½ teaspoons dried yeast (usually one packet)
½ teaspoon salt
250ml/9 fl oz lukewarm milk
170g/6 oz sugar
1 teaspoon vanilla extract
1 egg
7 tablespoons butter
100g/3 ½ oz sugar
9 tablespoons butter

Method
Put the 600g/21 oz plain flour in a mixing bowl and make a dip in the centre, sprinkle the dried yeast into the hollow and add the warm milk along with a pinch of the sugar. Let the mix sit in a warm place for 15 minutes.

Then add the salt, the egg, 7 tablespoons butter, vanilla and 170g/6 oz sugar and mix together (I do this in a food mixer fitted with a paddle). Mix until the dough is smooth and holds together. Add a little extra flour if you need to.

Place the dough into a greased bowl and cover, let it rise for 30 minutes.

Roll the dough out to about ½ inch thick on a lightly floured board and transfer to a roasting tin/tray bake tin (10 x 15 inches), gently squish the dough to fill the tin right to the edges.

Let the dough rest for a further 15 minutes. Pre heat the oven to

350F/180C/Gas 4.

Make some dips all over the top of the dough with your finger or the back of a spoon and sprinkle over the 100g/3 ½ oz of sugar (it looks like a lot, but it is OK I promise). Cut 9 tablespoons butter into small chunks and sprinkle those evenly over the dough as well.

Bake in the oven for 25 minutes or until the cake is done and the sugar mixture has melted with the butter and caramelised a bit.

Eats well cold with a cuppa or warm with custard.

Spice muffins (vegan)

All the spices of a pumpkin pie, but in a muffin.

Ingredients
350g/12 ¼ oz plain flour (all-purpose flour)
250g/9 oz sugar
1 teaspoon baking powder
½ teaspoon bicarbonate soda
1 teaspoon salt
2 teaspoons mixed spice
1 teaspoon ground ginger
250g/9 oz pumpkin puree
250g/9 oz coconut milk
110g/4 oz vegetable oil
2 teaspoons cider vinegar
2 teaspoons vanilla extract

Method
Preheat the oven to 350F/180C/Gas 4.

Line two cupcake trays with paper cases, you should get 16-18 from this recipe.

Mix together the flour, sugar, baking powder, bicarbonate soda, salt and spices. In a separate bowl whisk together the pumpkin, coconut milk, oil, vinegar and vanilla. Pour the wet ingredients into the dry and whisk until combined, be careful not to over mix.

Spoon the mixture into the cupcake cases, about two thirds full. Bake for about 18 to 20 minutes.

Sprinkle cookies (vegan)

These are not only pretty but absolutely have to all be eaten in one go...well that's what happens in our house anyway. If you only try one vegan cookie, make it this one.- I guarantee it will change your view on vegan baking.

Ingredients
300g/10 ½ oz plain flour (all purpose)
1 teaspoon baking powder
¾ teaspoon bicarbonate soda
½ teaspoon salt
3 tablespoons sprinkles
200g/7 oz sugar
100g/3 ½ oz vegetable oil
60ml/2 fl oz water
1 teaspoon cider vinegar
1 teaspoon vanilla extract

Method
Line two baking trays with baking parchment.
Mix together the flour, baking powder, bicarb, salt and sprinkles.
In a separate bowl mix the sugar with the oil, water, vinegar and vanilla.
Add the wet ingredients to the flour mix and stir until combined.
Scoop out a tablespoon of the dough and make it into a ball shape, pop it on the tray and press it down a little with your hand to flatten it slightly.
Once you have all the cookies out on the trays, pop them in the fridge for an hour. This helps them to keep their shape once they are baking.
Pre heat the oven to 190C/375F/Gas 5.
Pop the trays of cookies into the oven and bake for about 10 minutes. They will puff up slightly and be very lightly

coloured on the bottom.

This recipe should make about 12 cookies.

Coconut truffles

These look like snowballs...

Ingredients
200g/7 oz condensed milk
175g/6 oz desiccated or shredded coconut

Method
Put the ingredients in a bowl and mix together. Using your hands mould the mixture into walnut size balls placing them on a baking sheet. Pop the truffles into the fridge for half an hour to set.

Digestive biscuits (cookies)

My son loves to make and eat these biscuits.

Ingredients
250g/9 oz flour (white or wholemeal)
250g/9 oz butter, cut into cubes and slightly softened
250g/9 oz medium oatmeal
75g to 125g/2 ½ oz to 4 ½ oz soft brown sugar - depending on
how sweet you like them
2 teaspoons salt
2 teaspoons baking powder
About 1 tablespoon milk

Method
Rub the flour and butter together until the mixture resembles
fine breadcrumbs (or pulse them in a food processor). Add
the oatmeal, sugar, salt and baking powder and mix together
adding a little milk a few drops at a time until it all comes
together in a sticky dough.

Dust with some more flour and wrap in cling film and chill for
about 30 minutes.

Remove from the fridge about an hour before you want to roll
it out.

Dust the dough with flour and roll it out, dusting regularly with
more flour to stop it sticking until it is about 3-4mm thick.
You might find it easier to roll it out between two sheets of
greaseproof paper dusted with flour.

Preheat your oven to 180C/350F/Gas mark 4

Cut the biscuits out with a 6-7cm cutter and transfer them to
baking sheets lined with baking parchment. Bake for up to
10 minutes. Check regularly after the first 5 minutes. They
should be golden brown around the edges and lightly
coloured on top.

Spice bombs

These are little cakes filled to the brim with warming spices. Eat them as they are, warm from the oven they are very special or slice in half and spread with butter or jam.

Ingredients
150g/5 ¼ oz golden syrup
150g/5 ¼ oz soft brown sugar
150g/5 ¼ oz butter
4 eggs
400g/14 oz plain (all purpose) flour
2 teaspoons bicarbonate of soda
4 teaspoons ground cinnamon
2 teaspoons ground cloves
200g/7 oz sultanas

Method
Preheat the oven to 180C/350F/Gas Mk 4.

Over a low heat melt the golden syrup, sugar and butter in a pan. Leave to cool a little then add in the eggs, mixing after each addition.

Next stir in the flour, bicarbonate of soda and spices. Once it is fully mixed together add in the sultanas and stir again.

Butter a 12-hole muffin tin and spoon a dollop of mixture into each hole. You only want to fill each one up to about halfway. You may have enough mixture left to do another half batch. Don't overfill otherwise they will explode over the top and that won't be pretty.

Bake for about 20 - 25 minutes.

Mulled wine hot chocolate

What could be a better combination? Wine and chocolate?

Ingredients
400g/14 oz sugar
200g/7 oz cocoa powder
2 cinnamon sticks
5 star anise
8 cloves
500g/1 lb dark chocolate, chopped
2 satsumas cut in half (leave the skin on)
1 sprig rosemary
1 bottle of red wine
500ml/1pint water

Method
Put the water, sugar, cocoa powder and all the spices into a saucepan and bring to just before boiling.

Remove from the heat and add in the chocolate, whisk until it is all mixed in.

Pop the satsumas and rosemary into the pan and leave to infuse for about ten minutes.

Add the red wine and heat gently for a few minutes - serve warm.

The Basics

Here I wanted to share some of the basics that can have all sorts of flavours added and used to create any type of dish. It just needs a bit of imagination.

Yorkshire puddings

These light and fluffy British traditions are fabulous served with a roast dinner, but can also be made and filled with chilli, casserole or stew. In Yorkshire where they hail from, they are also apparently eaten spread with fruit jam…

Ingredients
150g/5 ¼ oz plain (all purpose) flour
2 eggs
150ml/5 fl oz milk
110ml/3 ¾ fl oz water
Salt and pepper
Beef dripping, lard or vegetable oil

Method

Pop the flour in a bowl and beat the eggs into it gradually incorporating the water and milk as you go.

Season with salt and pepper.

Pre-heat the oven to Gas 7/425F/220C.

Add a blob of fat or a dash of oil to each section of the muffin tin or roasting tin and put it in the oven to heat the fat for about 5 minutes until the fat has melted and become hot oil.

Carefully lift the tin out of the oven and pour the batter in.

This makes about 9 individual muffin size puddings or one large roasting tin size.

Bake on the top shelf for about 25 minutes until they have risen and become crisp and golden.

Options

You can add herbs, mustard powder or spices to the batter but also add the magic by serving it with gravy, sauce or syrups.

Stack (American) pancakes

I have included chocolate stack pancakes in this book, but here is the basic plain recipe.

Ingredients
225 grams/8oz plain flour (all purpose)
1 tablespoon baking powder
1 pinch of salt
1 teaspoon sugar
2 large eggs (beaten)
30g/1oz butter (melted and cooled)
300ml/10 ½ fl oz. milk

Method
The easiest way to make these is to put all the ingredients into a food processor and whizz. But it is easily done in a bowl with hand whisk. Make sure you beat it until there are no lumps.

Heat a griddle or pan.

Drop spoonfuls of the mixture onto the hot pan. Once you see bubbles coming up and blistering on the top it is time to flip them over and cook the other side - they will only take a minute or two on each side so keep an eye on them.

Serve warm with syrups, butter or juice. Or eat cold spread with butter or jam.

Options
You can add flavourings into these such as chocolate chips, spices or herbs but you can also bring in the magic with the toppings that you serve them with.

Pizza

A pizza base is a perfect background to add in all sorts of wonderful magical ingredients if you fancy something savoury rather than sweet (personally I would have both...).

You can buy packets of pizza mix that you just add water to, but it is really easy to make.

Ingredients

300g /10 ½ oz strong bread flour

7g (2 level teaspoons) fast action dried yeast

1 teaspoon salt

3 tablespoons olive oil

175ml/6 fl oz warm water

Method

Pre-heat your oven to 240C/475F/Gas 9.

Combine the flour salt and yeast in a bowl and then gradually add the oil and water, mixing together to form a soft dough, it will be slightly sticky.

Dump the dough onto a floured surface and knead for about 10 minutes (or 5 minutes in a mixer with a dough hook).

Divide the dough into 3 equal pieces then roll them out nice and thin. Place them on greased baking sheets then add your toppings.

You can go with the traditional tomato sauce, but I like to use a white béchamel sauce instead.

Once you have added your toppings bake them in the oven for 8-10 minutes

Traybake sponge cake

Use this sponge recipe as a blank canvas, adding in different spices, fruits or even herbs. Tray bakes are brilliant as they are simple to make and excellent to cut up and use for rituals or celebrations.

Ingredients
225g/8 oz butter, softened
225g/8 oz sugar
275g/9 ¾ oz self-raising flour
2 level teaspoons baking powder
4 large eggs
4 tablespoons milk

Method
Pre-heat your oven to 180F/Gas 4/350F. Grease and line the base of a 12 x 9-inch baking or roasting tin.

This is an all in one recipe so all you have to do is pop all the ingredients into a large bowl and whisk them together until combined. If you are adding spices, fruit or herbs stir them into the mixture at this stage.

Pour the mixture into your prepared tin and bake in the oven for 35-40 minutes. Leave to cool in the tin then cut into pieces.

Options
Add in a handful of sultanas, dried cherries ordried apricots.
Add a teaspoon of ground cinnamon or ginger.
Pop in a handful of chocolate chips.

Pastry (shortcrust)

Ingredients

Plain flour (all purpose) - 350g/12 oz

Margarine or butter - 250g/9 oz

Water - about 3 tablespoons

Method

This is an easy method; you just rub the fat into the flour and then stir in a little of the water at a time until it comes together as a dough.

You can use wholemeal flour, but you might need a little extra water.

A slew of slaws

Coleslaw is a personal favourite and it can be made with all sorts of veggies. Mix and match with what you have in the fridge, experiment and see what flavour combinations are your favourite.

Ingredients
One medium white cabbage, sliced
3 carrots, grated
150g/5 ¼ oz mayonnaise
2 tablespoons cider vinegar
Salt and pepper to taste

Method
Mix it all together...simple.

Options
Add in a tablespoon of mustard.
Mix in a teaspoon of chilli flakes.
Mix in a teaspoon of fennel seeds.
Mix in a teaspoon celery seeds.
Mix in a teaspoon of mild curry powder.
Replace one of the carrots with a grated courgette (zucchini).
Replace half the cabbage with grated celeriac.
Use half white cabbage and half red cabbage.
Add in half a grated red onion.
Throw in some sliced spring onions.
Add in a handful of sultanas.
Replace the cider vinegar with lemon or lime juice.
Add a handful of mixed seeds (pumpkin, sesame, sunflower).

Bread making tips

Bread can be a bit tricky, so here are some tips to help sort any issues.

Remember that yeast is a living thing, it likes warmth to active it and help it grow.

When you add yeast into your bowl of flour keep it on a separate side of the bowl from any salt that you add, until you mix it. Salt can kill yeast.

Knead for a decent amount of time, a good rule is ten minutes by hand or five minutes in a mixer with a dough hook. Test the dough, if it is nice and springy and has a smooth surface then it is a good dough. Prove in a warm place, if the bowl and the room is cold, it will take forever to rise. I put mine in the conservatory if it is a warm day. During the winter I often pop it by a radiator, or beside the cooker if the oven is on. Proving should take on average between one to two hours for the dough to double in size. Knock back after the first prove, gently knead the dough again to knock out any air bubbles. Prove again, the second prove is usually shorter, somewhere around 45 minutes.

Gluten free: Gluten is found generally in wheat flour although there are some very good gluten free flour blends on the market you can also bake with alternatives such as rice flour, buckwheat flour and coconut flour (to name a few). Some of these react in a similar way to wheat flour, others such as coconut flour must be handled in a very different way.

Flour can be substituted for meal, such as corn meal but bear in mind that it has a coarser texture and is best used in things like cookies and brownies. Rice flour and buckwheat can make a slightly sticky and more compact textured cake than usual. Adding in some ground almonds helps lighten the mixture.

Buckwheat flour: We have eaten excellent crepes in France made with buckwheat flour, but it works well for pastry and cakes as well. It will give your cake a darker colour and a denser structure than wheat flour.

Chickpea flour: You often find this in savoury Asian dishes, but it can be utilised in baking particularly for batters and puddings, it works best in cakes when combined with other types of flour.

Coconut flour: You will have to experiment with this one but as a very loose general rule for every 3 cups of wheat flour you will only need ½ to ¾ cup of coconut flour. Coconut flour sucks up all the liquid like a sponge (no pun intended). Recipes that use coconut flour often require a larger amount of eggs than usual as well, they are needed to bind the ingredients together properly.

Cornmeal and cornflour: Cornmeal in its coarse form is often called polenta which can be made into savoury dishes. Look for the finer cornmeal to use in your baking which works well in cakes and breads. Cornflour is totally different (sometimes called corn starch) this is not used for baking but for thickening sauces.

Gluten free: Most supermarkets now stock gluten free flour which is usually a blend of different flours mixed together such as brown rice flour, potato starch and tapioca flour.

Make your own gluten free flour blend:

This makes 9 cups of flour.

Mix together 3 cups of brown rice flour with 3 cups of white rice flour and 1 ½ cups of arrowroot powder and 1 ½ cups of potato starch.

I have tested various ready-made mixes with a lot of success. Most of them already have xanthan gum added which helps the texture of the finished bake. You can buy gluten free bread flour mixes which turn out really well. For most cake recipes you can just substitute an equal amount of gluten free flour (check that it has xanthan gum already added), but it may be a bit of trial and error.

Nut flour: You are probably familiar with using ground almonds in cake mixtures and it works very well. It does give quite a strong almond flavour and a denser cake. Hazelnut flour works well in cake recipes too.

Rice flour: A good all-round flour that doesn't have an overpowering taste. Works well for pastry and in batters. Add in some brown rice flour to give it a better structure.

Tapioca flour: Reminiscent of school dinners, I actually love tapioca pudding. This is a really good flour to use in puddings, cookies and batters.

Xanthan gum: This sounds horrible but is actually added to a lot of gluten free recipes to add structure and help bind together the ingredients. Some of the store-bought gluten free flours already contain xanthan gum so check the packet before you use it. It can make some recipes a bit gummy but see what you think. If you want to avoid xanthan gum you can try flax meal mixed with water.

Vegan baking

What does this mean? If you are baking vegan style, then you cannot use any animal products or bi products such as eggs or dairy so these need to be replaced. Baking is a bit of a science so you may have to do some research and experimenting to find the best results.

Dairy free: I find dairy substitutes for milk and butter much easier to deal with than gluten free flour.

Butter can be replaced with some margarines (check the ingredient label to make sure it doesn't have animal fat in) or try using vegetable or coconut oil. Dairy milk can be replaced with almond, rice or soya milk. Coconut milk works the same but will give a slightly coconutty flavour to the dish. I have used all the milk alternatives in lots of different recipes, and it seems to react in exactly the same way dairy milk does and can be used as a direct substitute. To make your own buttermilk just add a 1 tablespoon of lemon juice to one cup of non-dairy milk.

Egg free: This is slightly trickier; I have found it to be anyway.

Some recipes use vegetable oil instead, but have a look around on the net, there are a lot of recipes that you can use.

Flax is a good suggestion. To replace 1 egg, you will need 2 tablespoons of finely ground flax meal mixed together with 3 tablespoons of water. Let the mixture sit for ten minutes so that it thickens up. Then add to your recipe in place of the egg.

Applesauce is another good substitute in place of eggs, use 60g/2 oz of applesauce for one egg. Mashed banana works in a lot of recipes such as cake loaves and pancakes, use half a banana in place of one egg.

Aqua fava is a very good egg replacement. It is a fancy name for the liquid you find in a tin of chickpeas. When whipped with sugar the aqua fava can actually be made into meringue. Three tablespoons of aquafaba is equivalent to about one whole egg, while two tablespoons of aquafaba is equivalent to about one egg white.

Honey free: Honey is a bi product of bees, so for vegan baking will need to be replaced. A good substitute is maple syrup or agave syrup.

Conversions

Although I live in the UK and most cook books and recipes give the weights in grams I love using the American 'cups' measurements, it is so easy. If you get stuck on the weights, here is a conversion chart:

Liquids:

Fluid Ounces	USA	Imperial	Millilitres
1	2 tablespoons	2 tablespoons	28
2	¼ cup	4 tablespoons	56
4	½ cup	8 tablespoons	110
5		¼ pint	140
8	1 cup		225
10	1 ¼ cups	½ pint	280

Solid:

Ounces	Pounds	Grams
1	28	
2		56
3½		100
4	¼	112
5		140
8	½	225
12	¾	340
16	1	450

Oven temperatures:

Fahrenheit	Celsius	Gas Mark
275	140	1
300	150	2
325	170	3
350	180	4
375	190	5
400	200	6
425	220	7
450	230	8
475	240	9

Dry goods:

½ cup = 4 ounces

1 cup = 8 ounces

2 cups = 16 ounces

Ingredients

Some of the ingredients we use daily have different names in different countries, here are the basics:

Plain flour = all-purpose flour

Corn flour = corn starch

Icing sugar = powdered sugar or confectioners' sugar

Aubergine = eggplant

Courgette = zucchini

Strong white flour = unbleached flour

Spring onion = scallion

Single cream = light cream

Double cream = heavy cream

Full fat milk = half and half

MOON BOOKS

PAGANISM & SHAMANISM

What is Paganism? A religion, a spirituality, an alternative belief system, nature worship? You can find support for all these definitions (and many more) in dictionaries, encyclopaedias, and text books of religion, but subscribe to any one and the truth will evade you. Above all Paganism is a creative pursuit, an encounter with reality, an exploration of meaning and an expression of the soul. Druids, Heathens, Wiccans and others, all contribute their insights and literary riches to the Pagan tradition. Moon Books invites you to begin or to deepen your own encounter, right here, right now.

If you have enjoyed this book, why not tell other readers by posting a review on your preferred book site.

Recent bestsellers from Moon Books are:

Journey to the Dark Goddess
How to Return to Your Soul
Jane Meredith
Discover the powerful secrets of the Dark Goddess and transform your depression, grief and pain into healing and integration.
Paperback: 978-1-84694-677-6 ebook: 978-1-78099-223-5

Shamanic Reiki
Expanded Ways of Working with Universal Life Force Energy
Llyn Roberts, Robert Levy
Shamanism and Reiki are each powerful ways of healing; together, their power multiplies. *Shamanic Reiki* introduces techniques to